Pearls of Faith

Pearls of Faith

A Forty-Day Devotional

Regina McIntosh

Foreword by Keith Blankenship

RESOURCE *Publications* · Eugene, Oregon

PEARLS OF FAITH
A Forty-Day Devotional

Copyright © 2025 Regina McIntosh. All rights reserved. Except for brief quotations in critical publications or reviews, no part of this book may be reproduced in any manner without prior written permission from the publisher. Write: Permissions, Wipf and Stock Publishers, 199 W. 8th Ave., Suite 3, Eugene, OR 97401.

Resource Publications
An Imprint of Wipf and Stock Publishers
199 W. 8th Ave., Suite 3
Eugene, OR 97401

www.wipfandstock.com

PAPERBACK ISBN: 979-8-3852-5331-9
HARDCOVER ISBN: 979-8-3852-5332-6
EBOOK ISBN: 979-8-3852-5333-3
VERSION NUMBER 10/23/25

With all my heart, I encourage you—dearest reader—to read between the lines of this work and discover the faith that brought this effort to completion, the faith that is mustard seed faith, the faith that taught me to always listen to the still, small voice who silences the doubts inside each heart who loves Jesus, the reason I am writing these words.

Pearls of Faith would not be without the love that God sent to me in the form of a mother, a grandmother, a husband and all the many friends who have been such gentle blessings to my spirit. But, more than anything, I am reminded to give credit where credit is due, *especially*—I'm so thankful for the Holy Spirit, who has guided each morsel of faith that touched these pages and I would like to thank Him and my Jesus, the God who created me, for every thought that made a way for Pearls of Faith to be.

Written with a heart who has been encouraged and inspired by faith in Jesus, who is still writing my story as I seek to worship through my words and poems. I'm placing my faith in His hands as I remember each blessing—especially HIM, my Savior—and my husband, Morris McIntosh and my mother, Norma Riddle—and all the other family and friends that have blessed me with their love and prayers. I'll always thank God for His blessings who have made my life a better one.

He Has Only Just Begun
By Regina McIntosh

On swift wings, blessed by the light,
who pours out the melody,
scriptures come to life—in the song,
joyful noises, crafted by hope,
soothing away the dark, coloring the life
in gentle truth, praises poured out,
all through the music, songs drifting,
on the edge of a heart—rhythmic, beyond the winds,
who remember only the showers,
the storm who haunts with its whisper,
blessings gesture to the souls who recall...

on swift wings, they soar, gliding through the skies,
at peace with the graceful sun, at peace...
they seem to sing, 'just see what God has done',
"J U S T S E E... what God has done...

And, He has only just begun! He has only just begun!

Contents

Foreword by Keith Blankenship	ix
Introduction	xi
Day One	1
Day Two	4
Day Three	7
Day Four	10
Day Five	13
Day Six	16
Day Seven	19
Day Eight	22
Day Nine	25
Day Ten	28
Day Eleven	31
Day Twelve	34
Day Thirteen	37
Day Fourteen	40
Day Fifteen	43
Day Sixteen	46
Day Seventeen	49

Day Eighteen	52
Day Nineteen	55
Day Twenty	58
Day Twenty-One	61
Day Twenty-Two	64
Day Twenty-Three	67
Day Twenty-Four	70
Day Twenty-Five	73
Day Twenty-Six	76
Day Twenty-Seven	79
Day Twenty-Eight	82
Day Twenty-Nine	85
Day Thirty	88
Day Thirty-One	91
Day Thirty-Two	94
Day Thirty-Three	97
Day Thirty-Four	100
Day Thirty-Five	103
Day Thirty-Six	106
Day Thirty-Seven	110
Day Thirty-Eight	113
Day Thirty-Nine	116
Day Forty	119
Conclusion	125

Foreword

In the book of Hebrews, Chapter 11:1, we read that faith is the substance of things hoped for, the evidence of things not seen. By faith, the elders obtained a good report. Through faith we know that the world was formed by the word of God. So things that were not formed were created and molded by the hand of God. By faith, we know all these things.

It's sad to see today that so many are putting their faith and trust in things that are merely idols, false gods forged by mortal hands—gods that are not gods at all, but phony and fake replicas of what people create from their own desires and dreams. They are nothing close to the amazing and glorious God of heaven, the God who writes our stories with pens of grace and faith.

Those who know God and have a good understanding of faith, know in their hearts that there is only one God and He is the God of the bible, the God Johovah who is the maker of heaven and earth and all that is or will ever be. He is the answer for those of us who yearn for love that lives eternally, love without pretense or doubting, love that abides with each one who believes He is who He says He is.

In Psalms 19, the bible says that the heavens declare the glory of God, and the firmament showeth His handiwork. The earth is filled with His glory. For me, if nature was His only testament to His amazing strength, His nature, His peace—proof that He is the only God we will ever need, that would be enough.

But there are so many other proofs of Him, His grace and peace, His gentleness and blessings, His gifts to each of us who

Foreword

worship at His cross. All anyone needs to do is seek Him to find the peace that surpasseth all understanding. He is the ONE and ONLY God who brings hope to those who simply believe in Him. In faith, we have the opportunity to know what it means to love beyond our own abilities, to see beyond our own hopes, to share in a love that means we'll forever be filled with faith that is simply another blessing from God.

The bible says the just shall live by faith. If a heart desires joy and peace, love that completes, in this life—the only way is to trust, have faith, in the One who created the heavens and earth, the One who created each heart and soul. He is the Prince of Peace and the King of Kings. The Lord Jesus Christ is everything to those who share in this faith He stirred in each of His followers.

Regina has written another book for the Pearls Series, *Pearls of Faith*, and I believe this work will encourage and inspire readers. If you take a moment to read through this work, I know you'll find a glimpse of the faith that shines through its pages.

>May God bless all of you.
>Yours in Christ,
>Pastor Keith Blankenship
>Fox Creek Baptist Church

Introduction

Genesis 50:20 "But as for you, ye thought evil against me; but God meant it unto good, to bring to pass, as it is this day, to save much people alive."

I met a woman I'll call Doubt. Doubt resembled me in some ways. She liked to read. She seemed interested in protecting children and animals. But there was something about Doubt that caused me to wonder. Was she a Christian? Did she know the love of God? Was she Jesus' follower? I had to know.

When I first started a conversation about God with Doubt, I was met with an adamant "NO. I do not believe in God! I am an atheist." Atheist! Atheist? Oh, my. I was in for trouble. Despite every reason I had for not following directions when God told me to work His name, His Son's name and Christianity into my conversation with Doubt, I did it. These were unwelcome thoughts I'd placed in the mix for Doubt. Soon, she was letting me know – without any doubt, that my God thoughts were unwelcome.

Hmmm? Could it be that Doubt doth protest too much!? Hmmm?

Finally, I came to realize that I was only stirring the pot, so to speak, with all my meanderings and ramblings about the Lord. Doubt wasn't biting. But, Doubt did love to read. I decided I would offer her one of my books of Christian poetry. As soon as I handed over the volume she retorted, "I won't read it!" "Oh," I told her, "it's poetry." As if she wouldn't have realized that but from my soft reply

Introduction

she seemed to have relaxed a bit. "Ok," she said simply, accepting my token and placing it in a place for later examination.

Just before placing my book in Doubt's hands, I felt the Holy Spirit prompting me to recall that verse that I wasn't apt to think of on my own at all. The verse that says, Matthew 7:6 "Give not that which is holy unto the dogs, neither cast ye your pearls before swine, lest they trample them under their feet, and turn again and rend you." Yes. My books certainly were my small pearls. But, was God telling me to ignore the sinner's heart, the one who needs saving, the one who I felt determined to plant my seed of Him inside? Surely not.

After offering my book to Doubt, and going on about my day, I heard a message that reminded me we have all been those 'swine' at some point in life. Each of us had to hear about Jesus and each of us had to have the opportunity to believe Him. Doubt is no different than me. Yes. Her sin is different than my own, but her need for a Savior is not different at all.

Just after this I was separated from my friend, Doubt. She went her way and I went mine, but I have not one doubt that my ministering to her was well spent. She might not meet my Jesus. She might not get saved. She might go to hell. But, not without my prayers. Not without my sincerely planting the seed that I hope has taken up root in her spirit. Not without the friend who believes, believing that she is indeed one of the souls who has heard the gospel here on earth. She might not take the initiative and become a Christian. But, how am I to know?

I threw my "Pearls" before swine and I believe the One who inspired me to write those words has blessed me all the more, with blessings only my heart can sing of, because – in spite of their dark heart, I ask Him to save the atheist as well as the believer. We are all sinners. We all need a Savior. And, thanks to God, to Jesus, to the blood, we have the freedom – even in our sinful state – to repent, reach out and rest our souls in His embrace. I'm so very thankful that He made a way that only love could have paved. His road is the road to eternal hope, eternal faith, eternal grace. His road is the road to everlasting peace and I am walking this road when I seek

INTRODUCTION

to serve the ones that He sought when He came to live, die and rise again. Thanks to Jesus, I am surer than I've ever been that each tear I cry for the lost is a tear that stirs heaven's light so that it reflects what it means for God to silence all fear with His gentle strength.

There is nothing on earth that can change a heart. But when you mention Jesus, you can change the darkest heart. You can change the color of a thought. You can change the fate of what was lost. And, that – my friend, is worth the cost of your service to God.

I hope and I pray, that with these "Pearls" I've written from my heart, there will be one changed so that they'll reach that place where God can take away all their worst and give them a new heart, a new body, a new home in heaven, where He will forever abide with us.

All Doubt aside, let love be the guide! Let love be the guide!

Day One

Jesus loves you

Romans 1:17 For therein is the righteousness of God revealed from faith to faith: as it is written, The just shall live by faith.

There have been so many times I've heard, "you have such a good heart" or "you are kind and good". I beg to differ. My heart is far from good and I am not kind or good. I am a dreadful enemy many times, an enemy to the faith and an enemy to my own self. I am, at times, the very one who destroys the gifts that God bestows on my life. I act like an antagonist or adversary to the faith instead of a friend or ally for the God I love. Sometimes, I act like God's greatest warrior, while other times, I act like God's greatest rival. I am not good and I'll say it one more time, I am not good. I am a sinner with a dark and vile heart.

But, I am a sinner who believes in a Savior and, through the faith that He gave me, the faith and grace that saved me, I know that I am accepted by the God who made me to love the way He loved when He sent His one and only Son to live and die and rise again, so that His love could save anyone who simply has the faith to reach out and take His hand, believing in the One who died for every man. Thanks to this man, this Jesus who is the whole reason I can feel anything resembling love, I know what it is to believe, to have faith, to be justified because He is the light that shines from my soul, the soul He saved because He gave everything to save me from the enemy. He saved me and replaced the cold, hard heart inside of me with a heart that hears His voice, a heart who listens to His glory, a heart who knows that I'm far from good. Yet, because of Him, my faith in Him protects me from the weakness' that makes me human and keeps me from being good on my own. Because of Him, some people think I'm good, even though I know they're so wrong. Any goodness they see in me, is the goodness that comes from Him living in me.

Justified, YES. I'm justified by faith, the faith that He gave me, the same faith that saved me and the same faith that keeps me from giving up or giving in to the sins that taunt me and haunt me. Thanks to the wonder of His birth, the miracle of His cross and the gift of His resurrection, I know what it is to love more than I ever imagined possible, with a love that only He could have stirred inside my spirit, a love that is His for the asking and the giving.

And, because of the faith He gave me when He saved me, I know what it is be good, to be righteous in God's eyes, because I have faith in Jesus, my Savior, my everything, the most beautiful love that I've ever experienced. Thanks to this One I call Jesus, I know what it means to be justified by faith. Thanks to Him, I am saved to the uttermost and someday, I'll go home to heaven to be with Him forever! And, YES—oh YES. It is amazing!

A Prayer and a Promise

Dear Lord, I know You have given me a gift far more amazing, far more blessed, far more worthwhile than any gift that I've every imagined. Thanks to the love that saved me, the faith that made a way for me, I know that YOU will forever answer when I pray and You will forever be the hope that guides my way. Thanks to YOU and the faith you stirred in my soul, I know what it means to love without conditions, to love without expectations, to love in such

Day One

a way that I know—this love could only come from You, the One who loves beyond anything I could ever think of, with a love that I can't describe or explain because it is more beautiful than anything that has ever been. Thank You, Lord for giving me this faith and for saving me from a darkness I can't fathom. You are the One who I will forever praise with praise and conviction that remembers— You are the King of Kings and it is through faith in You that I know the calm of a peace that takes away all my fears and reassures me that You're the whole reason I'm here! I love You, Jesus!

> Faith is a living, daring confidence in God's grace, so sure and certain that a man could stake his life on it a thousand times.
> —Martin Luther

Day Two

James 2:18 Yea, a man may say, Thou hast faith, and I have works: shew me thy faith without thy works, and I will shew thee my faith by my works.

Faith brings salvation. Saving faith brings works, even though everyone knows souls aren't saved by works. When someone is truly saved, their lives will reveal their faith through the works that they demonstrate. James never says that a soul is saved by works. And, everyone knows this is not the case. But, after faith has saved, the saved will reveal their saved state by the works that they display. It may be simply shown through some kindness or generosity. It may be shown through some talent or gift the Father has given them to use for His glory. It may be through missionary trips or gospel preaching efforts. It could be through serving others in simple ways that most will never see or know about. It might even be heard in the prayers prayed for others, prayers that reach the heart of God, our greatest reason for anything we undertake.

James is stating a simple fact that is still happening in today's society, maybe even more so in today's society. Christians like to quote the verses that assure us we are saved because we believe, because of our faith. They don't want to look past that point of believing and remember the other scriptures, the ones that tell us—once we're saved, we should be doing something other than surviving, something more than merely working for our best interest, something greater than just selfishly increasing our own wealth or treasure. I sincerely believe, as the noted scripture expounds on, we should be working for Jesus. We should be reaching out to others with the gospel, stretching out our hands to bless and provide, grasping other hands with hope, faith and love.

Because we've been saved from a devil's hell doesn't mean we should just sit back and relax, waiting for the time when we move into our mansion in heaven. God wants us Christians to go above and beyond what the rest of the world does. He wants us to seek that which is lost and give from the depths of our hearts. He wants us to show, through out own lives, that Jesus Christ is who He says He is and He'll do what He said He'd do. God wants us to show a lost and dying world the way out of the dark, the way out of hell, the way to touch God's heart and find the reason that shines light over everything that was once in the dark.

I know that there are so many people who will answer this verse with arguments like, but . . . we're saved by believing, not working. Yes. That is so true. We are saved by believing. But how can we even say we have a heart if we don't care enough about our fellow man to try to keep him or her out of hell? How can we honestly believe if we don't try to carry the gospel into the world where others can find the grace that we've received. How can we be true Christians if we don't tell others? How can we really imagine we're redeemed if we don't share the gospel? How can we be saved if we don't work—not so we'll be saved by works, but because we want the rest of the world to reach the same destiny we're moving toward. A destiny of heaven, where we'll finally meet the One who lived and died for us, face to face, where we'll finally praise Him forevermore, with praise that resonates through the heart and soul?

A Prayer and a Promise

Dear Lord, I know I don't have to work in order to meet You face to face. I know I don't have to struggle with the day to day tasks that are given me. I know You won't leave me or forsake me because of my working or not working—but, God, I also know that I want to praise You and please You. I want to show You what You mean to me. I want to give something to You that will remind You I'm Your child. Would I even know You, Lord, if I didn't want to show You my love? Just like little children often draw their simple pictures and give them to those they love—I want to give something to YOU, the greatest Father, my One true love. Even though the gifts I give are rather humble and don't reflect nearly the elaborate joy and vision that are carved into those gifts You give me, I sincerely believe that (just like an earthly Father would be) You are pleased with the things I offer You, the gifts that are from my heart and soul. I want to work, Lord, because I sincerely want to show You that I love You with all that I am. I love YOU, Jesus! You're my heart's greatest need, my soul's only need, the reason for everything I believe or deem worthwhile in my life. You are the inspiration in my smile, the light of my world, the reason that I love!

> Pray as though everything depended on God. Work as though everything depended on you.
> —Saint Augustine

Day Three

Hebrews 11:7 By faith Noah, being warned of God of things not seen as yet, moved with fear, prepared an ark to the saving of his house; by the which he condemned the world, and became heir of the righteousness which is by faith.

Having faith, sometimes means looking ridiculous to those around us, the ones who don't understand the instructions God has given us. They don't hear the voice that speaks into our hearts, the beautiful that inspires us to listen with a pure heart, the miracle of a love that restores our spirits when we're feeling like the worst of sinners. Having faith, sometimes means that we can't explain the roads we're taking, the journeys that, to others, might look misleading, the prayers that assure us—when in doubt, the One who listens will destroy the darkest doubts and help us to find our way through the shadows.

Faith led Noah to build an ark even though everywhere he turned, everyone who knew him doubted his reasoning, even his very sanity. As Noah worked, erecting this thing that no one on earth had ever seen, this thing that no one on earth had ever needed or had a reason for assembling, there were probably some insecurities going on inside this man who God had given the work of saving the human race and all the animals from extinction. Uncertainties assuredly breathed their weary words through Noah's mind. Hesitancy broke through his faith and tried to steal his peace. Even though Noah trusted the Lord more than anyone else on earth at the time, there were probably moments when Noah felt like he must be crazy because, after all, everywhere he turned there were those who swore that he was crazy.

Crazy and determined like so many others who have gone out on a limb that looked like it was close to the breaking point. Despite all the doubts, the fears that clouded the hopes and the tears that worked their way through the suspicions that were a part of the devil's plan to destroy God's design, the crazy and determined often discover that—with faith there is a way where no way can be seen. Through faith, there is a sense of promise, a reason, a feeling that through this wonderful gift from heaven, prayers are being answered with "YES". Thanks to the faith that sustains and brings hearts through the worst of pains, there is a promise that never fails, a beautiful that never fades, a light that wilts the darkest doubt and makes a way for the weakest soul to find the strength to reach beyond the fears and tears, rising above whatever suspicion might cling to the spirit.

Thanks to Noah, the one who taught us about faith that never gives up, there is a world where each of us are given the chance to reach beyond our doubts into the faith that promises we can make our way out of the worst that comes. We have what it takes—through faith, to silence the skepticism and know that, because of the Creator of our souls, the answer to our yearnings, we can face any fear, any doubt, any worry with the peace that comes from knowing God is always there. He is alive in every prayer. He feeds every heart. He erases every thought of giving up because He is the one and only reason that our hearts are beating. He is the love that lives to save us from the sin that made us afraid, the sin that wanted to take us away from the faith, the faith that sustains and the faith that remains God's greatest gift to us, the gift of His love.

A Prayer and a Promise

Dear Lord, You know how insecure I can be. I worry and doubt. I yearn to find a way out of the things that You give me to do because

Day Three

I'm so sure I don't have what it takes to do those things You say I can. I am often worried that I'm not enough, even when You promised that You would strengthen me with Your spirit. I know that You are with me and You will never leave me. Still, worry presses in around my hopes, my dreams, my prayers—silencing the truth that says, You are the answer to my every doubt, my every fear, every tear. Because of You, the faith that You gave me, I can make it through the darkest nights, the fiercest storms, the deadliest harm. Because I know You, Jesus and have faith in Your strength, I can overcome whatever comes, even when I don't think I can. You are the miracle that assures me, through faith, I can obtain the victory. Thank You, Lord, for the faith You stirred in me, faith that reminds me without You, I'm nothing at all. Without You, I am lost and alone. Without You, Lord, this world has won. I love You, Jesus and will always praise You for all You've done!

> Faith is deliberate confidence in the character of God whose ways you may not understand at the time.
> —Oswald Chambers

Day Four

> Galatians 2:16 Knowing that a man is not justified by the works of the law, but by the faith of Jesus Christ, even we have believed in Jesus Christ, that we might be justified by the faith of Christ, and not by the works of the law: for by the works of the law shall no flesh be justified.

Salvation is the only thing that gets us on the road to heaven, avoiding that horrible place where only nonbelievers are destined for. That place called hell and that place that many refuse to even believe exists, is the one place I want to avoid at all costs. And, I hope to show as many others as God allows me to the detour away from that tragic future.

The one thing that we all need to escape hell is Jesus Christ, the Lord and Savior who came into this world to save those that were lost, to restore hope and love, to bring peace with God. Thanks to Jesus, all we have to do to escape hell is believe in Him, the One who died on a cross so we might reach beyond our fears and tears into the promise of eternal life. All we have to do is believe! Believe in the One who gave hope to the most frantic, the most miserable, the most lost souls on this earth.

Faith is the one thing it takes to reach beyond our fears, to rise above the tears and to leave our doubts in the shadows of those past years. Faith makes a way out of the darkness, a way through the loneliness, a way that reminds us that—YES! It is finished. Jesus

Day Four

spoke those words many years ago from the awfulness of an old rugged cross where He hung because our sins were so dark we'd lost all hope of finding our way back to God, restored and redeemed. Because our sins were so black and ugly to the One who created us, we would never be able to share eternity in His presence.

But, Jesus paved the road to heaven. Because He came to earth and never sinned, never—not even once. He was innocent and therefore, able to save us from the torments of a place called hell. Because HE knew no sin, our sins can be forgiven. Because HE died blameless, our hearts can be saved. Because HE was spotless and so completely filled with LOVE, we are able to reach beyond the darkness of the grave—into the abundance of eternity with Him, the One who saved us from, not only hell. . . though that would be plenty enough—He saved us from the hatred, the depravity, the evil that resides in this world. He saved the souls of those who place their faith in Him from the failures, the faults, the wrongs that want to take us straight into the darkness that sin loves.

Faith—just believe. No amount of working for salvation will convince a Holy God to accept our hearts and souls. It is only Jesus who is capable of saving us from the sin that keeps us away from the very One who created us. Thanks to Jesus, we can know God and know love. Thanks to Jesus, we can know that faith in HIM, in His life, His death and especially His resurrection. . . built the foundation for our homes in heaven where we'll live with God eternally, in everlasting love and joy, peace and wonder, amazed by what He's done for us!

A Prayer and a Promise

Dear Lord, You know my heart even better than I know my heart. You know what I'm feeling before I feel it. You see beyond my thoughts to the source of my hope, my hurt, my happiness. You know me in a way that I'll never know me. And, thanks to You, I can feel loved by the grace that You've poured out over me and share in the faith that You gave so abundantly to those who would BELIEVE, simply believe, in You—the answer to our every need, the One who silences every dread, the reason that I can sincerely say. . . YOU are my everything. Thank You, Lord, for saving me and giving me hope that goes beyond optimism. This is a hope that anticipates the future I have with You, a future in heaven, a future that lasts forever. Thank You, Jesus. I'll love You forever.

> You were made by God and for God, and until you understand that, life will never make sense.
> —Rick Warren

Day Five

James 1:3 Knowing this, that the trying of your faith worketh patience.

It's in the testing of our faith, the trials, that we discover the strength of our faith. And, so does the Lord. He allows us to go through the trials and testing because He wants to prove our faith strong and reliable, revealing the faithfulness inside of us, the assurance and the endurance, the confidence that will remind us we have all we need if we have the Savior who will, one day, take us home to live with Him throughout eternity—always alive in our spirit, always alive and free to be the children of God that He permitted.

He is wise and in our most humble faith, we can be sure that His love, His grace, the faith that He gave us will sustain us. It is a saving faith and it is a faith that He roused when He saved us from that awful place where unbelievers will someday know that they've made the mistake of choosing darkness over light, doubt over belief, Satan over God and hell over the happiness of heaven where we'll live throughout eternity, forever sharing in the wonder of life with the King of Kings, the Prince of Peace, the joy and peace, the love that is alive and will reflect the wonder of His light throughout eternity.

I'm so very thankful that He is mine. He is the reason that I survived the trials I've known and He is the reason I will survive the trials that come. He is the answer to my every prayer and He is the faith that sustains me so that I know He's there. He is the miracle of abiding peace, the tenderness of grace, the music in my heart when I cling to His hand, the feeling of love that assures me He is always there and He will always care. I've never known a time when I couldn't confide in Him and I've never experienced a moment when I wasn't able to cling to His hand. I'm not always sure of myself. That is certain. But, I'm always sure of Him and that is even more certain.

Faith like this is meant to be tried and tested so that, when all is said and done, we can be even more certain that God is the One we're leaning on. He is the One we can depend on. He is the One we can confess our worst sins to, knowing that He will forgive in spite of the dark place we've been. He is the One who listens to our prayers without reminding us that we don't deserve any of the blessings we've had. He never makes us feel like we can't come to Him with all our needs, our dreams, our trials and our temptations. With a heart full of hope and a spirit full of faith that He stirred, we can lean on the One who answers us when we pray, the One who cares for us when we're afraid, the One who smiles when we praise. Thanks to HIM, we never need to know what it feels like to go to that awful place called hell and thanks to HIM, we never have to spend one moment alone and afraid. Thanks to this amazing Savior, we have all we need, all the faith that it takes, to enter paradise with the assurance that we are assuredly in the place where only love can take us.

I know there will be tests of my faith. I know there will be trials and some of them will break my heart and tempt me to doubt. But, I also know there is someone I can go to when these times come. I know there is a man called Jesus who is making intercession for me and I know, beyond any doubt, that He will make a way for me to walk away from these tests of my faith with the assurance that He is with me and He will never leave me. I can always run to Him when I need a true friend and He will always be there, willing to lead me through the trials and place me on the road to victory. Without Him, I would be lost. But, with Him, despite the cost, He assures me that this faith will sustain me.

Day Five

A Prayer and a Promise

Dear Lord, I know that You know me better than I know myself and I haven't a doubt that I've lost out many times because my faith wasn't strong enough or I didn't have the trust it takes to pray when I should have. I know that You know all of this and still, You make a way for me to reach beyond the shadows of doubt and cling to the hand You're holding out. Thank You, Jesus, for guiding me home when I come to You with all of my doubts. Thank You for letting me know, with YOU, I am never alone. With You, I have all I will ever need to be sure that love is alive and I'll survive whatever trail comes. I love You, Lord and will be forever grateful for the faith that You gave to me.

> Faith is deliberate confidence in the character of God whose ways you may not understand at the time.
> —Oswald Chambers

Day Six

Jesus loves you

Mark 11:22 And Jesus answering saith unto them, Have faith in God.

Jesus cursed the fig tree, which withered away. When Peter brings this to Jesus' attention in this verse, He tells Peter to have faith in God, explaining further in the next verse that whosoever shall say unto this mountain, Be thou removed, and be though cast into the sea; and shall not doubt in his heart, but shall believe that those things which he saith shall come to pass; he shall have whatsoever he saith.

These are powerful words. If we believe, truly believe—we can have anything we ask of God. We can have that same wisdom that Solomon sought. We can have the inspiration drawn from David's hope, the hope that inspired his kindness, his love, the beauty in all his psalms. We can know what it is to believe the way Abraham did. We can silence every fear with a faith that is clearly more alive than any faith we might have imagined we'd share in when we first came to Christ.

This is the wonder, the invaluable wonder, of knowing the Jesus who walked through the valleys, crossed over the mountains

Day Six

and even walked confidently on the sea. He is the Savior and He is the reason that I know faith can take me into the presence of One who created the world and, also, created my soul. He is the Father of love and He is living in heaven with the saints He raised up. He is the reason that I know what it is to believe and He is the center of this faith that silences every doubt I might have conceived.

When I was younger, my faith wasn't as strong as it is today. I often questioned the bible and this Jesus who most of the people I knew claimed held the answers to every fear, the comfort for every tear, the tenderness that would keep me filled with assurance and hope. Most everywhere I went here in the bible belt, I found those who had faith and shared that faith without an inkling of doubt. They assured me, that whatever I faced, whatever demon might darken my heart, discourage my hope or erase my dreams—with Jesus by my side, I had all that I needed to come away from the sorrows and struggles with my faith intact. I didn't understand that kind of strong faith the way I do today.

It took years of trouble—despair that wouldn't leave me, heartbreak and grief, feelings that left me sure I didn't have the strength to face tomorrow or the possibility of another day with the resistance of doubt that followed me and held me with its solid grasp. Yes, I was afraid. I was alone. I wasn't living on a prayer at all. I was living on the tiniest hope, the smallest belief, the least faith that I could have felt. It wasn't like I didn't believe in Jesus. It was simply like I didn't believe I was worth His time or His cross. I didn't think I had the right to reach out to the One I had always ignored and discounted. I didn't realize how badly I needed Him or how much He yearned to heal me of all that sin I was carrying around with me.

Finally, after seeking and pleading and believing—assurance came to me. Assurance that this man named Jesus had truly saved me and, even though I had plenty of sin to be regretful of, I had plenty of love that He placed in the new heart He gave me when He saved me. And, I realize—even now, that this faith He stirred in my soul will never let me go without the assurance of the One who touched me with more love than I've ever experienced before.

Thanks to Jesus, this faith that He placed in me is leading me to follow after Him, always amazed and always sure that wherever I'm taken, whatever road I go down and whatever trouble I'm facing, He is there beside me—the light that abides in me, replacing all that sin I had with a beautiful that can only be HIM!

A Prayer and a Promise

Dear Lord, You know me and You know, better than anyone, how difficult it was for me to finally let go of my way so that I could discover the way You made, the road You paved, the miracle of this faith that would take me out of the sin filled life I lived into an astonishing wonder, a place that You stirred in my soul, a place where I endlessly sing of Your love. You amaze me and I'll forever praise You with a heart who is yearning, aching, longing for the heaven that awaits when my last day on earth has been lived and I'm finally there with You, where my heart has always been. Thank You, Jesus, for everything You've done for me—this child of God who wasn't always capable of giving You the honor and glory You so deserve. I love You, Jesus and will always be grateful for the faith that sustains me.

> I am still far from being what I want to be, but with God's help I shall succeed.—Vincent Van Gogh

Day Seven

> Luke 7:50 And he said to the woman, Thy faith hath saved thee; go in peace.

When I read that verse, my thoughts are a very heartfelt . . ."Thank God I'm saved!" This, yes, this is the reason that I can write these words without being overwhelmed by the flood of light pouring out in my spirit, the flood of hope raining down through my feelings, the flood of grace that frees me from being lost in the unending need to regret all those sins that I've partaken of. Oh, yes, I regret. But, thanks to this Jesus who saved without restrictions, I can rest in the security of my salvation, the security of knowing that He saved me completely from every last sin, every last offense, every last fault. He saved me and I'm free to write about the grace He gave to me, the same grace that made me worthy of the hope that sustains me, the hope of heaven where I'll remain with Him throughout eternity, forever alive—throughout all time.

Thanks to Him, I know how it feels to be that woman who was made whole. I know how it feels to be released from the darkness that was so overpowering it had me reaching out to the worst temptations, the worst depravities, the worst evils, because it took a while for me to realize that all I had to do was go to the One who died on the cross so that I wouldn't be lost in this despair or disgrace. Thanks to Him, I know how it feels to be pulled out of the muck and the mire that was sucking me into its depths. I know how it feels to reach out, timidly, and have the most incredible love fill my heart. This is the grace that replaced all my doubts and left me with the assurance that I finally know the light that will never flicker and go out.

He told that woman from so many years ago that faith had saved her. Faith! That is a big word from a big God who gives BIG LOVE to those who will simply listen to His invitation and take the hand of the One who created them. It is faith that makes it possible to move from the darkness of sin and sorrow into the light of peace and promise. It is faith that destroys the fears, silences the tears and reassures hearts throughout the years. It is faith that humbles and faith that saves and faith that is measured by the hand of God Himself. Faith is alive, a prayer breathed inside, who remembers that, through believing, we have the chance to know the very One who shined that light into our hearts. This faith is a sustaining faith and it calms every anxiety, making the heart to feel the calm—the peace that comes to the soul who believes and finds the victory from being saved by His unending grace.

It was faith that made a way and it was faith that gave me enough hope to pray to be saved. It is faith that remembers to thank Him for His salvation and it is faith that silences my doubts when I'm overthinking. This faith that He gave me is the reason that I'll one day sit beside Him in heaven, overcome with the joy that must be like a flow of love falling from His glory. His love will, one day, surround me in a beautiful that I can't hope to even imagine. Because I believe. Because I have faith, I can know beyond the shadow of a doubt that love will always make a way out of the darkness, bringing souls to the new joy, the new glory, the newness of a love that is impossible to ignore or reject. This is love that clings to the very soul. Because I have faith, I know what it is to share in this love that overshadows every other love.

A Prayer and a Promise

Dear Lord, Thank You so very much for saving me, for making me whole, for shining Your light into the darkness that was my sin

Day Seven

shadowed heart. Thank You, Jesus, for making a way for me to pray and a way for me to say—I'm saved to the uttermost. I'm saved from the past and I'm saved from all doubt. Thanks to the faith that You stirred within me, I know what it is to be free from every sin. I love You, dear Lord, with all that I am and I can never stop thanking You for all the joy You've inspired within me. With all my thanks and all my heart—this praise I give is forever, eternal, endless.

> Resist your fear; fear will never lead you to a positive end. Go for your faith and what you believe.
> —T. D. Jakes

Day Eight

> Titus 2:2 That the aged men be sober, grave, temperate, sound in faith, in charity, in patience.

Instructions for elderly men to be 'grown-up', to be 'honorable', to be 'decent'! Yes. That is surely what we all need more of. Then and now, we need real grown-ups, really honorable and decent human beings who are capable of sharing their morals, maxims and message with those who are just starting out in life. Through the elderly, we learn what it is to live respectably, wholesomely, honorably. Through the elderly, we SHOULD be learning these things. Sometimes, needless to say, our older generation fails to share the light that we are seeking when we're young and just starting out in life. Many times, it takes a few errors in judgement to finally happen upon a heart who is wise and warm and willing to share with us the paragon for living that we're so in need of. Sometimes, it takes looking past the most obvious choice (possibly a father or mother) and looking toward someone we've met along our way. Maybe a preacher or a teacher or a coach.

It's hard to say before we come across them who will be that exemplary model for our lives unless we've been blessed with family who are flawless. It's usually the case that we, especially those closest to each other, are met with the sins and faults in our moms or dads or other family members which make it almost impossible to place them in the role of mentor or advisor. Most of the time, even if we do have exemplary family members, we'll go beyond our

Day Eight

families to the outside world to discover people we admire and can embrace as guides. Though this isn't always the case, many times it is. Hopefully, though, we find men and women who encourage, inspire and challenge us to be shining lights for the God who created us. Hopefully, we can become men and women who will one day be the lives a younger generation seeks to hold to as examples. Hopefully, we will one day be the mentors we sought in others. It is definitely something to encourage and pray for.

When I was young, I met a few women I looked up to and valued. Some of them were quite admirable and fully deserved my respect. Others, I must admit, weren't nearly as worthy. Still, I found my way, more often than not, toward the women who were reliant on Jesus as their Savior and friend. It would often take the shape of kindness, caregiving, creativeness and friendly behaviors. Their grace, which had been planted inside by the hand of the Master, was extended to the heart I had and the faith that, even then, made me lean toward those who loved the Lord. Even though I had many struggles to encounter in my future and many troubles that would nearly destroy me as a young woman, there was always something within me that sought Jesus in others and, I believe, sought after HIM, His love and His peace, the joy of knowing the One who would eventually win my heart, my soul and my worship—my very best. This is what I hope to always give to Him—my very best.

It's also true that, today, I hope with all my heart that I can be a light for the ONE who gave me the answer to every doubt, the hope that never fails, the serenity that is forever kind and the wonder of a love that never burns out. He will never leave the heart cold and He will never fail to free the imprisoned soul. He is the Savior and He is more than just beloved. He is the whole sum of real LOVE. Agape Love. True love! May HIS LIGHT fill the whole world!

A Prayer and a Promise

Dear Lord, You know that I've made my share of mistakes and I've taken roads that I wish I'd failed to take. You know my sins, the ones that sometimes eat holes in my mind and take out bites from my hope. You know me better than I know myself and because You know me so well, I know that You know when I fail to let this light You stirred to life inside me—shine like it was meant to. Sometimes, I know that You look at me and see just how desperate a soul can be. Still, YOU LOVE ME! I can never stop thanking You, Jesus, for that love. Love that kindles up every dream I've every imagined. Love that sees me through the worst despair. Love that sings grace to me when I don't know how to let go of my sorrow. You are the One who makes a way for me, through all the darkness—You shine for me, a light that seeks me when I'm lost and a light that encourages me when I doubt. You are my life, Jesus. I love You more than my heart can express, more than my soul can voice, more than my life can utter. You are everything to me, Jesus. Everything I'll ever need. You are the love that sought me, bought me and taught me that You truly are my EVERYTHING! Thank You!

> Faithless is he that says farewell when the road darkens.
> —J. R. R. Tolkien

Day Nine

> Mark 4:40 And he said unto them, Why are ye so fearful? how is it that ye have no faith?

Storms rage, hearts quake, life takes a soul and leads it to and fro, like this sea who has flared up to fill the disciples, even disciples who are fisherman and well acquainted with the sea's outbursts and raging, with a panic that reminds those of us who know Jesus and His incredible power... to lean on His grace, through faith.

After the disciples wake Jesus to summon His help with the furious storm, He wonders why they still have no faith. He asks them why they're so fearful and how it is they have no faith? Jesus is attempting to instill a faith inside these men He chose that is stronger than any faith they've previously known, but He is astonished by their complete lack of faith as they show with their unbridled fear during this raging of the waters they're moving on.

Without faith, the heart comes undone. It trembles and quakes. It tumbles into the surmounting fears, the deafening darkness, the penetrating anxieties. Without faith, our lives aren't simply destined to failure. They're completely destroyed. Without faith, we're lost to the storms that break through our composure and fill our minds, our hearts, our souls, with a thunder that devours our contentment, devastates our solace and leaves our thoughts without the peace that once reassured our brokenness, our fear, our worries. Without faith, we're truly ruined.

It's faith that aspires to reassure. It's faith that rejoices when we're sure. It's faith that sustains when the brokenness tortures our hope. Faith leads us on paths of hopefulness, weathers all the worst storms and protects us from the doubts that linger in our paths when we give into the urge to mistrust the One who made a way where no way was. He is the only inspiration we need to believe. With Him, all things are possible and when He reveals His spirit to a soul, there is never any reason to fear.

I've known the feeling that comes over the spirit when it is living in fear. I've lived in fear, known the doubt—the trembling of suspicions, the reservations that once kept me from truly living. Because I once lived in fear, I can sincerely say that—with JESUS, there is no reason to fear. With Jesus, there is no cause for doubting or dreading. There is no motive for worrying or stressing. Thanks to this man who has the whole world in His hands, there is no fear that can succeed in tearing down the wonderful that He has written on the soul who believes.

Thanks to Jesus, I have left my fears in the past. Yes—I might feel inklings of fear now and again. It's scary to ignore that lonely call named fear when all you've ever known is to listen to its voice ushering you into the shadows that cling to anxiety. But, it is possible—thanks to the One who leads me. Because of Him, His love, His power, His assurance, I can cling to Him and avoid the darkness. Thanks to Him, I am blessed with a confidence that I've never known. With Him, there is refuge from every doubt. Insecurity can't touch me and fear can't extinguish the joy He rouses inside my soul.

Just have faith—believe! With Jesus, there is no need to fear anything!

A Prayer and a Promise

Dear Lord, Thank YOU for giving me the answer to my fear. That insecurity that once taunted me and kept me from reaching out and giving of myself is a insecurity that You silenced. Because of this faith I have in You, Jesus, I know the meaning of living life

Day Nine

to the full. Because of You, dear Savior, I can ignore those fears that once left me in the shadows and, clinging to Your hand, I can embrace the joy of knowing a courage that only You could have stirred inside me. Because I know You, Jesus, I know what it is to give of my heart, to express myself and to listen to the confidence that You gave me when You saved me. I love You, Lord and will be forever grateful for Your embrace, Your aid, Your grace and precious love.

> I have come to the conclusion that the most important element in human life is faith.
> —Rose Kennedy

Day Ten

Ephesians 2:8 For by grace are ye saved through faith; and that not of yourselves: it is the gift of God.

Have you ever prayed for God to save someone? I definitely have prayed that He bring salvation to family, friends and anyone who it is possible to save. I have prayed with the hope that, through grace, He will save the ones I love most and even the ones that hate me. I don't know about you, but I believe salvation is the one grace that can make this life worth living, make the heart worth the breaking and the soul worth the escaping from that dark place called hell. I don't want anyone to go to hell and I especially oppose those I love going to that awful destruction. Yes, I have prayed for God to save and I know that these prayers are making a way despite the fact that, in all truth—even though I'd surely love to, I can't save a soul.

No matter how much I love them or respect them or admire them, I can't save them. I don't have that power and the only One with the power to save is the same One who carried that cross so that everyone on earth would know His name, His way, the saving grace that reminds each one of us that the more we praise the more worthy Jesus is of that praise we're offering. Despite what our minds might say, our hearts and souls know that He is the only way and through faith, through grace, He is the only power who can save us from the outer darkness. Thanks to Jesus, His kindness and mercy, His unending love and grace, I can say that I'm saved to the uttermost and I have the hope of a heaven where I'll live with Him forever. Praise God!

Yes, for sure, I've heard myself and other Christians say that they would 'save them if they could' and there isn't a doubt that they would do just that if it were a possibility. But it is not. Even though we're saved by grace, through faith, we don't have the power or muscle to save another soul. Only Jesus has that power. Only Jesus Himself can reach into a heart and pull out all the darkness, all the doubt, all the bitterness and hate. Only Jesus can make a way through the pain, the sorrow, the fears and tears. Only Jesus has the wisdom or ability to control our fate with the salvation that writes our names in the book of life. If your name is there, you will never have any reason to fear. And, even though we might hope someone else will choose the Savior, we can't force them to get saved.

But, we can pray. Yes. Oh, YES! We can pray and praise. When we can't do anything else to save a soul, we can pray for the One who writes the stars in the skies, the One who writes our names in the book of life, the One who writes His light inside our souls—to change a heart, to mend a soul, to save someone to the uttermost. And, HE and ONLY HE can do it. Even though me and you aren't that powerful, we know someone who is that powerful, someone who can bring peace that surpasseth understanding, someone who grows light from the night and sheds hope across a life that had once been doomed. Because we know a Savior who can, through our prayers, we have the opportunity to change someone's destiny and the possibility of glimpsing the joy of a soul who is turned from doubting to faith in the One who created us to believe!

A Prayer and a Promise

Dear Lord, I know I don't have the power to save, but because You saved me, I do have the power to pray and I know that You hear me when I ask You to save someone dear to me or even someone who is an enemy. Because I know YOU, my precious Savior, I know that I can pray with confidence in Your healing, Your grace, Your gift of salvation that will change the destiny, the eternity, of me and everyone who chooses to follow You, the One who rewrites hearts and souls. Thanks to You, dear Lord, I can know that there is the chance for me and others to reach beyond this world into the eternal where You are forever writing love. Thank You, Jesus, for saving me and thank You for answering my prayers prayed with faith that You can make a way for others to know You, too. I believe You for this saving grace, the grace that changes destinies, the same grace that saved me and the same grace that will save anyone who chooses You, my Savior and my friend, the One who forgives every sin. I love You, Jesus. With all my praise and worship, I bring You each prayer with the faith that You will make a way for the willing.

> Oh, it is wonderful to know that our Heavenly Father loves us—even with all our flaws! His love is such that even should we give up on ourselves, He never will.
> —Joseph B. Wirthlin

Day Eleven

Jesus loves you

Hebrews 10:23 Let us hold fast the profession of our faith without wavering; (for he is faithful that promised).

F ears taunt me and haunt me. Some days, they won't leave me alone. And, somedays, I refuse to listen to their distinctive voice, a voice of doubt and shame, a voice of darkness and dread, a voice that destroys my hopes and dreams. Somedays I don't listen to them. But it is those other days when I hear them and heed them that silence my faith and remind me that I am, after all is said and done, only human. Thus, I am incapable of making it through the storms, the sorrows, the shadows that seem to come upon me all at once—when I let fear's voice dissuade my heart. Yes, sometimes I let fear's voice discourage, talk me out of my faith, deter me from the belief that is like a light to my dark.

But, other days—those days when faith lights the way for me with love to shine through the darkness, I remember that it is HIM, the One who remains my best friend through the good and the bad, who holds my hand. I never have to worry or fear. I never have to doubt the promise that is clearly my hope's assurance, my faith's promise, my life's guarantee that, when all is said and done, I will break through the doubt and reach the goal that I've been aiming toward. That goal is my relationship with the Savior, the One who shows me the way to love, the wonder in the word wonderful. He is alive and He helps me to survive the worst that comes. He shines light onto the darkest doubt and He sings joy into the deepest sorrow. He is my light and my life and my love. He assures me that, with Him, I never need fear the outcome. He is always just a prayer away and He will always save the day.

Everyone knows fear. It may come in those moments just before speaking and erase the mind, leaving a blank page for the voice to oust. Or, it may come in those times when a walk through the ally means passing by some unfriendly foes, those who know that you're alone and possibly just perfect for becoming the victim at the end of their gun. It might be from sickness or doubt. Fear might come from the divorce or the insecurity inside. It might come from knowing that sin has overcast the hopes and dreams, left its stain on everything and built a shame within the spirit that can't be mended without Jesus' intervention. Fear can come from so many places and it can silence some of the sweetest embraces. But, when it comes, there is always a place to turn.

Just turn to Jesus when fear whispers its lies into your mind. Listen to the Lord when fear tries to prevent you from revealing your heart and soul. Ignore the voice of fear when it taunts you with its endless dread. Believe in the One who made a way through every darkness and wipes away every tear, the One who silences each feat with the promise of a love that will leave huge holes in the doubts that once breathed panic into your faith. Hear the love that passes through the fear and remembers that you are His child and You can be brave, confident and bold. With Jesus beside you, you have everything you need to face the worst storms. There in the shadows, there lingers the beautiful story of the One who died for your soul and because He lives, you don't ever need to fear! He has this. Oh yes! He has this!

Day Eleven

A Prayer and a Promise

Dear Lord, Thank you for giving me so much to be thankful for. Your encouragement when I'm afraid, Your light at the end of the tunnel and Your promise that fear is a liar. . . all of these and so much more, I'm thankful for! Thank You, Jesus, for making a way for me when I felt like every direction would only bring sorrow. Despite my thinking, despite my doubting, despite my fear, YOU taught me that, with YOU, all things are possible and all I need to do is whisper YOUR NAME and I will have all the strength I need to face whatever fear comes at me. Thank You, Lord, for making a way for me when I felt like I was defeated and should have retreated. Thanks to YOU, I faced more than I thought I could and because You live, I can face whatever this life brings. I love You and praise You. You're amazing.

> I gave in, and admitted that God was God.
> —C. S. Lewis

Day Twelve

> Philippians 3:9 And be found in him, not having mine own righteousness, which is of the law, but that which is through the faith of Christ, the righteousness which is of God by faith:

Formalities and habits, traditions. . . can actually threaten our relationship with Jesus. It is FAITH and faith alone that produces the most amazing and abiding relationship with God's Son. It is faith that challenges our spirit, restores our soul and gives our lives the meaning that reveals Jesus in every part of our walk through this world. Wherever we are and whatever we're doing, we're most at home with Jesus when we allow our faith to take us to the places where He is best felt and most accepted. It is through FAITH that we can know the meaning of believing without limits. It is through faith that our lives are blessed in ways that can't ever be explained. It is through faith that Jesus gives us the victory when trials come. It is through faith that our souls are saved to the uttermost.

There is no virtue in me. I don't have any righteousness of my own. It is only the righteousness that comes from my faith in the Lord that gives me any reason to call myself God's child. Because HE is, because I believe, because of the faith that He gave me, I can know that I'm HIS. And, because I know I'm His, I can be certain that my faith in Him is the only virtue I have to speak of, the only feature that reflects His kindness, His grace, His amazing

Day Twelve

way. Faith in Jesus is the only way to enter into a relationship with God or to enter into the life everlasting that is given to those who have faith.

Needless to say, I've had doubts and I've been overcome by fear. I've known what it means to worry and have had anxieties destroy my hopes and dreams. But, despite the failures I've known and the shadows that have darkened my heart, there has always been the assurance that, with Jesus, I can find my way back home. With Jesus, I can let go of those worries and fears. I can find the victory that comes from knowing that, despite my doubts, Jesus will make a way for me and I will never be overcome by the darkness. Even when I am afraid I can be sure that He is there with me, inspiring me, enlightening me, inviting me into a close and secure relationship that is filled with love beyond my wildest dreams, love that blesses and fulfills and sees me through the worst there is. Even when I doubt, I still know that HE will see me through the sorrows and pains and restore my faith when I'm overshadowed by doubts.

There are times in every life when there is a lack of faith. That is just a part of being human. No one is perfect and there are fears, tears and even years when the heart is lost in trouble. Many times, it takes battling those doubts and fears, even struggling through the darkest dread and fighting away the sounds of skepticism and suspicion. There are times when we just have to remember that God is GOD and we are definitely not Him. We don't have what it takes to face those heavy battles without the grace that He reveals. We are not strong enough or wise enough or kind enough to make it through this world without leaning on the One who is more powerful than any demon we might face. Without Him, we are nothing. But, with HIM, we have all we need to face anything!

A Prayer and a Promise

Dear Lord, You know me and You know how I've struggled and how I continue to struggle with doubts some days. You know my heart and soul. You know the me that is weak and fearful and You know the me whose faith can take hold of those doubts that plague me and remind me that with YOU beside me, I have everything I need to face anything. Thank You, Jesus, for being my light, my strength, my life. Thank You for showing me that I can overcome whatever challenges come because, with YOU, there is no doubt that my soul is resting in faith that is everlasting, faith that brings me through the darkness and turns my worries into breakthroughs. Because of You, sweet Jesus, I am not afraid. Thank You. I love You more than anything.

> Believers, look up—take courage. The angels are nearer than you think.
> —Billy Graham

Day Thirteen

2 Corinthians 5:7 (For we walk by faith, not by sight.)

Sometimes I wonder what heaven will be like. Will it be, even a little, like the earth we know? Will there be trees and seasons, forests and streams, birds and bees? Will everything be different than what we currently see as such sweet peace? I wonder and I ponder, considering all the possibilities of what might one day, be a reality in the new life, beyond the misty spills of cloudlike mysteries.

There is no way to know what it will be like in heaven. It's impossible to see into that sweet destiny and know the meaning of everything biblical intended to amplify our interest in the sweet by and by. It may not be what we expect at all. It may not be forests and streams or birds and bees. It may not be anything resembling what we've seen in this world. But I have no doubt that it will be more beautiful, more enthusing, more amazing than anything we've ever seen on this earth. There isn't a doubt inside that shadows the light which will always be, the light of hope and peace, the light of a love that ever breaths sweet, the light of One who sings joy all through me, causing me to tremble with the ache of yearning for His presence. I may not know today what it is to visit heaven in the flesh, but one of these days I'll look at this moment and see that nothing I could have placed on this page—no amount of words or details, could have possibly brought to light the image that will be before me when I reach that magnificent destiny. Someday, I know there will be a great homecoming that I can't possibly describe or even imagine. It will be more wonderful than anything I've ever thought of and more humbling than any dream I might have fantasized. Without a doubt, one of these days, I'll know what it means to see into the greatest beauty I've ever seen and I'll praise in a way that will blend the music of my soul with His glorious light and love, the love that I can't even speak of without feeling an awe that is unspeakable!

Yes, I do wonder what heaven will be like. I even wonder who will be there when I arrive. Will I meet Jesus first? Will I bow down to praise the One who has held my hand throughout this life? Will I sing in a voice that is so melodious I could never have expected it to come from my soul? Will I feel the beauty inspired by the hope He whispered through me when He brought me home? Will I see my brothers and sisters in Christ—the ones who sang His praises throughout this life? Will I see my mom and dad, my aunt and uncle, my grandparents and great-grandparents? Will we all be together in the sweet by and by? Will I even remember the sins that darkened my heart when I was living on earth? Will I shine like the morning SON?

Only God knows what is to come. Me? I walk by faith—not by sight. Just like today's verse states. Just like today's living reverberates. Today I'm here on earth and I can't see what is to come but when I get there, love more alive than any fear will be waiting for me and, when I finally meet Him, I will be more myself than I've ever been on this earth. When I get to see the One who died for me and the One who I've spent my life yearning for, I'll be more alive than I've ever been, more alive than this life can dream. Thanks to the One I love forevermore, I know that heaven is my home and the only hope that will make my life of any value, my soul of any worth, my being any benefit at all. Thanks to my Savior, I can know this faith will silence all my fears and bring me the sweetness of heaven, where I'll live with Him who is sweeter than any friend.

Day Thirteen

A Prayer and a Promise

Dear Lord, It would be much easier to believe if we could simply SEE everything in our future, everything that You have prepared for those who love You. It would be easier, yes, but it wouldn't be to our benefit. We need to have faith, faith that You gave to every believer, faith that sees us through when we can't see the outcome, faith that prepares our souls for the moment when we finally see You face to face, feel the joy of letting go of all fear, all doubt, all the tears and letting Your love light our hearts and souls with a wonderful that we could never know without the wonder of You in our hearts. Thank You, Lord, for inspiring me to love, for stirring a hope in my heart and for encouraging me to always listen to the promises that You gave every soul who believes. I believe, Jesus and, thanks to the faith that sustains me, I know that—one of these days—I'll meet you face to face. Thank You, Lord, for saving me so that I can come home to heaven and eternal peace. I love You and praise You.

> I have not lost faith in God. I have moments of anger and protest.
> Sometimes I've been closer to him for that reason.
> —Elie Wiesel

Day Fourteen

Matthew 9:29 Then touched he their eyes, saying,
According to your faith be it unto you.

It takes faith to just live in the day to day. It takes faith to eat and sleep, to give and take, to smile and weep. It takes faith to gentle the darkness, to risk the heart, to inspire the hope. It takes faith to simply live your life. Without faith, everything becomes dark and dread takes over where light once assured thoughts. Without faith, echoes of pain press into the silences and cause the spirit to tremble. Without faith, there is nothing on earth that can erase the shadows who cling to the night and discourage the dreams that want to be freed so that faith can have her way and inspire the new day.

Jesus stirs faith in hearts who know that He is the reason for every light, every grace, every love. He is the answer to every fear, every tear, every apprehension. Without His grace, our faith has no place to go, no light to reflect, no hope to respect. Without Jesus, faith is without reason. He is the beautiful in each season. He is the blessing that frees us. He is the wonder and the purpose. His love is life for us. He is alive within us—those who believe and depend on His spirit to bring our faith to those we meet and spend our time with. Because of Him, there is faith that will never deceive, faith that calls out to the sinner, faith that gives without expectation of receiving, faith that results in hope beyond description. Because of the faith He gives, we can go anywhere at all and proclaim the

Day Fourteen

name of Jesus Christ, the One who made a way for us as we reflect the light He gave to us.

If we can simply believe, have faith that what we're praying for will be. . . I believe we can receive all that we've ever imagined or considered. Because of faith, we can know that our prayers will be answered by the maker of the stars, the tender of the earth, the creator of our dreams and the music in every soul. Because He lives, we can believe and know the meaning of faith that never lets us down, never flickers out, never leaves us without. With faith, we can move mountains and with faith, we can know all the answers He provides. His light and love never let us down. With Him, we have all we will ever need and more, so very much more.

Even though I can't say that I've never faltered, never wavered, from my faith in this amazing Creator, I can say that I've never felt like faith this alive would leave me in the sinking sands that can sometimes come around to make us feel like we're going to be swallowed up by a world who refuses to seek the love who makes life worthwhile. Because I know that He is with me, though, and because I know that He has forgiven me for all those times I've struggled with my faith and doubted and even betrayed. . . I can look up to the heavens and declare that beyond those stars, beyond those clouds, there is One who never lets me doubt more than what He can bless me with faith that knows no question, faith that is my heart's best blessing. Thanks to this faith that sustains me, I never will know what it feels like to go through this life alone, without anyone. Thanks to my faith in Jesus, I always have Him there to lean upon.

A Prayer and a Promise

Dear Lord, You are wise beyond what I can comprehend. You know my heart, my soul, my spirit. You know what I'm feeling even before I'm feeling it. You know what I'll do in every situation and You know who I'll be before I am free to believe I might be anything at all. You are the word that comforts my soul and You are the One who leaves me sure I can make it in this world where I sometimes feel like I can't go on. You are my life, Jesus and without You, my heart would sink into oceans of doubt where I'd most assuredly drown. But, because I have You and the faith that sustains, I can embrace the seas of shame and hurt with the knowledge that You have made a way for me, a way out of the heartache, a way through the sorrows, a way that is revealed in every truth that You spoke. I love You, Jesus, and can never thank You enough for giving me the faith to keep looking up!

> "Faith is the strength by which a shattered world shall emerge into the light"
> —Helen Keller.

Day Fifteen

> Galatians 5:22 But the fruit of the Spirit is love, joy, peace, longsuffering, gentleness, goodness, faith.

We recently celebrated Thanksgiving and my granddaughter told me I was always offering them 'stuff'—just little things that I hope would make them happy. Nothing really, but little things like little girls love, makeup or lotion, etc. Anyway, strangely enough, they'd come to stop accepting my kindness' and I wondered why. I told them to please accept my kind gestures because they were gifts of the spirit—gifts from my heart, small tokens of my affection for their beautiful gift to me.

My little granddaughter asked me, finally, "what do we give you?" and something that I remembered about us cherishing Jesus' presence instead of the presents at Christmas made me say, "Your presence!" That is what they gave me and what it is that makes my life worthwhile—a smile, a light that passes over the eyes, a gentle word, a kindness that often goes unheard. With their "presence" they provide me with the most beautiful gift of all gifts. . .

Love, that greatest gift of the spirit. Love that knows no reason or no season. It is always available and always giftable. It is love that makes life worthwhile and it is my little granddaughter's love that makes me smile when she comes to visit and offers me her "presence". Without this love, what in life would hold any meaning? It is love, that wonderful gift of the spirit, that accomplishes more in one moment than I can accomplish (with all my gifts) in a lifetime. The little things I give to her are just things. They don't mean a thing. They are only things. What means something is the feeling behind the gift. . . my presence is meant to share with her a love that she has stirred in my heart, a love that only the Lord could have brought to my life, a love that is more beautiful than any other gift on earth.

The greatest gifts, the fruits of the spirit,—love, joy, peace, longsuffering, gentleness, goodness, faith and all the wonderful Jesus gifts. . . they are the reason that I can honestly say, it is my family's presence that makes life worthwhile and leaves my heart with a smile. Thanks to Jesus, I know what it means to love without conditions or expectations. He showed me a love, agape love, that is beyond description. It is love that is everlasting and love that can't compare to anything found in this world.

Because of Jesus and this love He gives me, I can—in some small ways, give a bit of the wonder He gives me. Yes, I know better than anyone that love isn't in the gift. The love, you see, is in the giving. It isn't the gift that holds the meaning. It is the giving heart that holds the significance. Love of giving came to me from my family and Jesus is the biggest part of that family. I hope that I can, through example, instill this love of giving into the hearts of those I love and give to.

Even though my gifts aren't great treasures, I hope that— through a small token of my affection, I can put a twinkle in a eye, a smile on a face, a light in a heart. And, through my love, love that was stirred by the One who gave me the greatest love I've ever known, I hope that I can inspire another soul to give their heart to the Son.

A Prayer and a Promise

Dear Lord, I love You more than I can say, more than I can show, more than even I can possibly know. You are my life. You give me the best gifts of all—the joy, the peace, the grace. . . all the wonders that come from knowing You, the light of the world and the light that brought me out of the dark. You are the way to eternal peace

Day Fifteen

and joy and I will never be satisfied until I am there beside You, where You are the light that abides, the "PRESENCE" that makes everything right. Thanks to You, Lord, I know what it means to love without conditions and thanks to You, dear Lord, I will hope to always love others the way that You intended. Thank You, Lord, for all that You are and all that You've been and all that You are in eternity.

> God continues to work miracles in my life.
> —Willie Aames

Day Sixteen

Jesus loves you

Ephesians 6:16 Above all, taking the shield of faith, wherewith ye shall be able to quench all the fiery darts of the wicked.

I love the woods. Oh, yes, I surely CAN see the forest for the trees and it is amazing. It makes me feel like praising, praising the Creator of these wonderful woods, these oaks and pines, the feelings that arise during every excursion through them. Whether Summer or Autumn, Spring or Winter, I can find the joy in the season when I experience the season within the walls of trees that surround me when I visit the woods that encircle my home here in the mountains of Appalachia.

I would even risk saying that these old mountains are more than merely charming. They hold their own special charm that can silence the darkness and whisper a sweetness into the spirit that will cause even the oldest among us to feel a stirring, a thrill, an excitement that comes from strolling beneath the naked boughs of winter or the leafy branches of summer. Wherever you go, if you only walk a moment in the heart of these hills, there is a feeling that comes to the spirit, a spirit of joy unlike most feelings I've

Day Sixteen

ever known. It feels like the moment just before the morning sun explodes to kiss the dew covered rose or the moment when snow reflects the silence back to the heart who hears only the memory that it evokes. It feels like a dream, a hope, a prayer for what only God Himself could have whisked together with His clever spoon.

Yes, I surely do love the feeling that being in the woods creates inside me. It is almost as beautiful a feeling as the feeling that comes to me when I sit in the pew and listen to God's word being spoken and elucidated. It is almost like a prayer, but just not quite. Even though I love the woods and all the joy they can rouse within me, still. . . even those beautiful mountains with all their natural benefits cannot evoke a feeling inside like the feeling that comes to me when I experience the presence of Jesus, my Savior, at a church service—where I'm surrounded by other believers.

Just yesterday, in a little brick church called Bee Log, where my pastor was preaching about hope, I experienced a joy, a sense, a touch from the One who created the forests—the same One who created the pastors, the servants, the followers who meet together to remember that it is our FAITH, the shield that brings us so much comfort, which will free our hearts to love the woods without becoming someone who replaces our praise of the One who created those woods with praise of His creation, the woods.

I know so many who have done just that. They've replaced the praise they could be giving God from within the walls of a church—with the praise of whatever it is that gives them a good feeling, a feeling that is actually causing them to ignore God's command to gather with other believers and worship the One who created them. He didn't tell us to worship the creation, but HIM, the Creator.

Take up the shield of faith and remember that He is the answer to every prayer, to every care, to every fear and every tear. He is the reason we worship and He is the reason we can experience so much love for those beautiful woods He created. Yes, He is there amid the trees as well as being there in the church where we can feel His presence so strongly. Jesus is everywhere. But He didn't command us to gather together with the trees. In Matthew 18:20,

He told us, "For where two or three are gathered together in my name, there am I in the midst of them." He didn't say two or more trees. He said two or more followers, people, human beings. We are told to gather together and that is what makes up the church.

Take up your shield of faith and apply that shield when someone tells you that being in the woods is just as good as being in the church. I love the woods, too. But the woods are not the church and it was inside the church yesterday that I felt the presence of the One I love so deeply and completely.

A Prayer and a Promise

Dear Lord, I know I'm so very far from perfect, but—most thankfully—I know You are still working on me and someday, when I enter those gates to be with You forever, I'll be the soul You molded and formed, prepared for such a time as this. Thankfully, I can know, without a doubt, that You are making me someone that God can't resist. I love You, Jesus and praise You with all that I am. Thank You so much for taking hold of my hand, my dirty hand, and leading me quietly and steadily toward that promised land. Once I'm there, in Your care, I know I'll be cleaner (cleansed by Your blood) than I've ever been. I love You, In Jesus Name, Amen

> Oh, it is wonderful to know that our Heavenly Father loves us—even with all our flaws! His love is such that even should we give up on ourselves, He never will.
> —Joseph B. Wirthlin

Day Seventeen

Luke 22:32 But I have prayed for thee, that thy faith fail not: and when thou art converted, strengthen thy brethren.

There isn't a doubt that the devil hopes to tempt us all into hell with his lies and deceit. When the Lord tells you that HE has prayed for you, though, there isn't a doubt that you'll be able to overcome those lies and deceptions. Because of the prayers of the King of kings, there isn't any reason to stress. He will make you strong enough to withstand the evil that attempts to destroy you. He is wise. He is strong. He is good and He is that light that falls gentle amid the worst darkness the enemy can introduce to you. Thanks to Jesus, we don't have to fear the fiery darts of that old fiend, the devil.

When I feel tempted—by the shadows, temptations that come to me in the form of gossiping or anger, greed or skepticism, coveting or some frustration that irritates the self-control that keeps me on the straight and narrow—a smile forms in my heart because I know, even though I'm tempted, the One who loves me with a love that is more potent than any other love there is, fills me with the assurance, the grace, the faith that promises, whatever I face, He has made a way for me. Without any doubt, He is there with me, quieting my worst fears and reminding me that, with Him, all things are possible. Even overcoming the lures of that fiery serpent. Yes. With Him beside me, all things are possible!

Faith! Faith will never fail. Faith is a promise that when darkness falls, the light is just waiting to be flipped on. Faith is the gentle that whispers warmth into the cold, hope into the forlorn, love into the loathsome. Faith is the reminder that, with Jesus inside, there is nothing to fear. Nothing can harm us so long as we have the One who strung the stars, lit the moon and sun, reflects the music that the angels wrote. When we have Jesus, there is nothing in life or beyond life that can destroy the grace, the joy, the faith that kisses away every doubt we might face. With Jesus, there is no reason to question. With Him, all things are possible and even the impossible becomes promising, even probable, for the ones who know Him as Savior, Redeemer, Liberator.

Faith is a silent prayer, a glimpse toward the skies where our heaven rides, a trembling moment when all our worries are focused on the assurance that His love will make a way for even the worst sinner among us. Faith is that intimate promise that, in time, He will invite us into the presence of His light, His love, His lingering blessing. Faith remembers, despite the worst that comes, there is the assurance that, with Jesus—we have already won.

Never let go of the faith that He stirs inside those hearts who sincerely believe He is the One who came to make a way through the pain, the past, the parts of life that seem most capable of destroying the faith that will guide us. Never stop believing. Never stop seeing the wonders that He bestows, the reasons our lives are so full of hope. Never stop letting Him take your hand and lead you on toward the promised land. Never let go of the faith that will bring you through the darkest disgrace, the dreariest shame, the shadows that mistake your faith for folly and try to keep you from reaching out to the One who sprinkles life with His starlight.

Faith in Jesus comes with only one predecessor, the single most important sign that your faith is true—love that only the One above could possibly have stirred up in you.

Day Seventeen

A Prayer and a Promise

Dear Lord, You know me and my heart. You know when I worry and when I can't bury my doubts. You see me trembling when the tears burn through my senses. You realize that I need You even before I start to pray, pleading with You for the love that will make a way. Thank You, Lord, for giving me the faith to believe, the faith that sees, the faith that agrees with You, the reason that I will always pray for You to shine Your light into my heart, Your love into my soul. Thank You, Lord, for YOU, the One who stirred up this faith that reminds me, always, You are my eternity. You are my forever. You are the One who my heart needs and You are the reason I'll love without thinking, love without reason, love without expectation of receiving. Thank You, Jesus, for this miracle of faith, the faith that You gave me, the faith that made me give my heart and soul to You, my greatest love—my Savior.

> The dearest friend on earth is a mere shadow compared to Jesus Christ.
> —Oswald Chambers

Day Eighteen

1 Corinthians 2:5 That your faith should not stand in the wisdom of men, but in the power of God.

Nothing I can say will change a heart or soul. Nothing I can say will make someone think one way or another. And, nothing I can say will bring about salvation. My words are merely trinkets, like those found on the most beautiful Christmas trees, and they mean little when they're compared to the wonder of a star shining down from the top of the tree. Like the smallest ornaments, my words are often ignored as mere baubles and don't do very much to augment the beauty of the tree in the same way that the topper does—that topper being the King of Kings. Just like those small baubles, my words are simple and sometimes crude. I don't always know how to reveal the faith that sometimes wavers within my bosom. I don't know how to expose the wonder that causes my heart to tremble in His presence. I don't know how to divulge the mystery of One who is, sometimes, just too amazing to explain. He is enigmatic, bewildering, amazing, yet—the message of the gospel is so simple even a child can understand it. Even a child can grasp the message that I may fail to explain with my extensive selection of nouns and verbs.

The gift of Jesus is too big for wrapping paper and too wonderful for any plan of unwrapping with fumbling hands. This is a gift beyond our ability to describe. It is bigger than the sea and more powerful than the wildest tempest. It is the wonder that

Day Eighteen

breathes hope into souls and the amazing that kindles flames of faith within the heart who knows He is the Lord. He is the answer to those prayers prayed so sincerely that we come away from the praying with our faith revived. He is the friend who never falters or turns away from the darkest doubts that we find causes our souls to shudder, our hearts to wither, our smiles to hesitate in their twist from down to up. He is the way out of the fear. He is the truth that never despairs. He is the life that fills our souls with grace. With this gift called Jesus we have no reason to ever let anguish shadow our souls with doubt. Because of this man, God eternal, we can reach past the misery, the desolation, the gloom, into the center of a love that grows more beautiful with every moment spent in the presence of this light called Jesus, the only true King.

When I think of how I've neglected my own soul's yearnings to be close to the One who created me, an eternal being, a child who is allowed to enter into a relationship with the Father of every joy, every peace, every wonder... when I think of the ways I've disregarded that still, small voice, the voice of my Savior and my Creator, the voice who calms the storms and scatters stars wherever His heart plans to strew the music of starlight, I am completely speechless. If not for His light, His love, His grace, I wouldn't know the meaning of hope or the promise of salvation from the torment unbelievers face when they leave this world.

We all go out of this world—prepared or unprepared, and I haven't the words in my gamut to explain just how important the message Jesus brought to the world is. I don't have the words or the reason. I don't have the ability or the wisdom. I don't have it in me to heal or send the sinner's heart the conviction that only the Holy Spirit can.

God is the only One who can silence the doubt, hush the tear, quiet the fear. Only God, His Son and the Holy Spirit, are capable of making the redemption plan available to those who truly reach out in faith—faith that reminds the soul, with Jesus as that shining star, the star who came to us one silent night so long ago, we'll never need to face one moment without the hope that is undeniably, the greatest plan ever given to man. That plan, God's plan, for salvation is the reason I can honestly say that heaven will be mine someday!

A Prayer and a Promise

Dear Lord, You know my heart and soul and You provided the way for me to know a hope that is beyond describing, a hope that is so inspiring, a hope that is mesmerizing. Thanks to the love You gave me, the love that saved me, I can know, beyond the shadow of a doubt, that my life holds a meaning far better than anything I could have possibly done on my own. Thanks to YOU, sweet Jesus, I know that my heart has been blessed by the best blessing made available to someone who has sinned so vilely, so corruptly, so scandalously. Thanks to You, my precious Savior, I know that—despite all the sins I've known—I have a hope that is more beautiful than my pen can describe, a peace so provocative that I can't explain it, a love so wonderful it will never fail to amaze me. ThankYOU, Lord, for You and for the plan that is surely guiding me into the promised land.

> The man who radiates good cheer, who makes life happier wherever he meets it, is always a man of vision and faith.
> —Ella Wheeler Wilcox

Day Nineteen

> 1 Timothy 6:10 For the love of money is the root of all evil: which while some coveted after, they have erred from the faith, and pierced themselves through with many sorrows.

I watched "The Christmas Carol" just yesterday and was struck, for the umpteenth time with the reminder that the love of money, greed, surely is the root to so much evil in this world. Love of money causes friends to part, families to dissolve, hearts to be broken and wars to commence. The love of money is definitely a reason to respect those who remind us all to be generous, to give, to share a part of (not just our hearts and our lives) but also our earnings.

Generosity is something that comes naturally to some of us, while, for others, it seems like it takes them a lifetime to see beyond their bank accounts into the promise of a heavenly account where money means absolutely nothing. Money is a tool used to provide for those in need, to bestow hope to hearts who dream, to grant joy to those whose feelings bleed tears of loneliness and lack. Even when we fail to see past our own reasonings for keeping those bills in our wallets, we still know, deep down, that giving back—as there is no doubt God intends us to—is the purpose of our lives, our souls, our earnings. When we part with that twenty, there is little doubt that God's love restores to us so much plenty. We'll never outgive God.

While God's gifts of money and material possessions can be very nice, there is one gift that He provided us which nothing we can think of could ever bring more delight. While His love is amazing, this gift He gave to us is—wonder of wonders, peace and grace, the reason for joy and the reason for faith. This gift, His one and only Son, brought to earth a hope for eternity that no other gift of love could have spun. Jesus is the King of Kings, the whisper of peace, the light that smiles through all the world's greed. Jesus is everything to me and so many others who see Him for who He is, the LOVE that saved us from hell and torment, the LOVE that made us a part of His family, a child of our Father, God—forever.

The love of money is the root of all evil. It distracts our hearts from the real reason we're here—to give, to love, to breath hope into a dark and dreary world. It diverts our hearts from the miracle of a love that was poured out when Jesus' blood silenced all our fears. It confuses and complicates, causing us to forget the most important part of our life, the walk we take with Christ. The love of money confounds and depresses, muddles dreams and erases beliefs. It promises to give us only one thing—the world. And, it is the world we need to let go of as we find the miracle of life, the hope that comes from the flow of a love far more beautiful than any light, a love that came down to bring to us the glow that spreads God's fire, the love that is the answer to every need, every fear, every doubt. Love this amazing could only come from the One who breathed His love into our souls when He saved us from the death that would have wrecked our soul and left us without His presence, the reason that grace is so much greater than His many material blessings.

A Prayer and a Promise

Dear Lord, There isn't a doubt in my mind that the love of money surely is the root of all evil. While I hope and pray that my heart is focused on the right things, You and the love You have put into my soul, I know that there is always a part of me that will be tempted by this material world and the money that controls it. Even when I

Day Nineteen

feel sure that I can overcome, I know that there is still the possibility that I fall into the sin of loving money and I ask you to simply pull my heart away from those temptations that cause me to sin so blatantly. Thank You, Lord, for making my heart tender and keeping me from the love of money. Thank You, Lord, for showing me that when it comes to money, I need to remember that whatever I have and whatever I give, whatever I might own—it is yours. So, whatever comes, I hope that You will know, I'm so thankful for the generosity that You have bestowed on me and my family. I love You, Lord and I praise You, always, with my heart and soul, with the love that is truly my greatest blessing of them all.

> Faith is the bird that feels the light when the dawn is still dark.
> —Rabindranath Tagore

Day Twenty

Romans 9:32 Wherefore? Because they sought it not by faith, but as it were by the works of the law. For they stumbled at that stumblingstone;

When my heart faces something that I feel like I can't face, when my soul hides beneath a shadow of shame and disgrace, when time feels like this hour, this pain, will never pass—I am left with the only option I can choose to make a way through the demons that seek to discourage and dissuade. I am left with my Jesus, the One who paid the price for my past, the One who left me with His Holy Spirit, the One who made me into a woman that I could never have imagined myself being. Because of Jesus, I am someone that I couldn't have been. I am someone who believes the impossible and risks all that I have to find shelter beneath His wings. I am someone who has faith, faith that only He can give, and faith that makes a way for me to have a relationship with the One who created everything that is, including me!

And, even though I have faith, I do things for my Jesus. I let go of my bitterness and spite. I make my way through the doubts that cloud my mind. I seek out ways to give back because He is mine. I listen to His words when I feel like hearing mine. I reach out to those I wouldn't have sought because I know it is what He would want me to do. I go above and beyond the call of duty when it comes to love because I know,—Oh, yes. . . He went above and

Day Twenty

beyond, so far above and beyond that I can't possibly explain the way He gave His whole heart, His whole hope, His whole love. He gave so that I, when I go to Him with faith, can know the wonder of a love that mellows my darkest rage, turns my sorrow into hope, my suffering into growth, my frown into a smile and my worry into assurance that, with HIM, I can have the key to every door, the answer to every prayer, the faith I need to let go of my doubts and reach beyond those fears and tears into a pleasure, a wonderful, a blessing that will last me throughout all my years.

Some attempt to come to God by doing. They might give their money, give their time, give their promise to everything that is assuredly right. But, what they lack, what the heart needs, what brings righteousness that comes from the One who saves souls and brings true peace, is complete FAITH in the ONE who gave up His life, died as the ultimate sacrifice and came back to us—arose, so that we could have a hope that is beyond wonderful. This hope it the miracle that offers a promise of everlasting love, eternal peace, forever with the One who came and died for, not only me, but everyone who does the one thing needed—simply believe.

Our verse today says that the ones who tried to come into a relationship with God through works stumbled at the stumbling block. That stumbling block, the Lord Jesus, sacrificed all so that we could know the wonder of a love that frees our souls and leaves us with a promise that He'll never let us go.

When I find myself stressing over what I haven't done for Jesus, I remember that He gave me, in my heart, the one thing most needed. He gave me faith, a believing, that will always bring me through the worst that comes. Because I believe in Jesus, I have the assurance that, through Him, God not only acquits me from all of my sin, He blesses me with eternity where I'll forever be with HIM!

A Prayer and a Promise

Dear Lord, You know me better than I know me. You know when I doubt, when I work and don't listen to Your word. You know when my dreams are fading and You know how to make me see Your answers. You are the way, the truth, the life. With You beside me, I never have to worry that I'll let the darkness finish me. Because YOU said it is finished, I never have to know what the end truly is. Because of You, my precious Jesus, I know what it is to love without conditions, to give because You first gave to me. . . the love that healed me, the love that seals me, the love that reveals to me—everlasting grace, peace and light, the mystery of a love that keeps me assured I'm blessed beyond what I can comprehend, with blessings that only Your love could have sent. Thank You, Jesus, for everything You are and everything You'll forever be. I love You with everything I am. Eternally!

> God never made a promise that was too good to be true.
> —Dwight L. Moody

Day Twenty-One

Jesus loves you

Romans 4:5 But to him that worketh not, but believeth on him that justifieth the ungodly, his faith is counted for righteousness.

Though I may try, nothing on earth can I do, nothing—not one thing—that will make me a child of the King of Kings. My best work or works, my most sincere efforts, the greatest gifts I have to give. None of these will make a way to unlock the doors of heaven and allow me to enter there when I've left this earth and all its sorrows.

The only way to Jesus is through faith in Him who lit the sun and struck hope into the lonely souls. It is only faith in the One who came and died and rose again that will rebirth my soul and make me a child of the King of Kings. Only faith has the ability to invite me into a relationship with the One who reflects the music God placed in my heart. Only faith can lead me to the love that comes from the brightest Son. Only faith can restore my hope for more than this world, the hope that abides because faith never subsides. Only faith can see through the shadows of doubt, into the light of a soul who knows that Jesus is the answer to every darkness.

Jesus is the reason that my life has meaning. Jesus is the welcome home that reminds me, though I was lost, I'm found and He will be at the door when, one day, death raps its knuckles and I finally answer despite the fear I'll undoubtedly have. Despite all the worries, the dreads, the doubts—it is faith that guides me past the suffering and sorrow, into the joy that abides in tomorrow.

Working for the Lord is definitely a good thing. When someone gives, from the heart—when someone provides a teacher, a preacher, a reacher for the Holy Spirit, it is amazing and wonderful and a blessing. It is a gift that often means our faith is working. But when a heart uses the work, the giving, the preaching or teaching, with the thinking that this work they're doing gives them some secret key into a special relationship with Jesus or a secret key into heaven, there is no basis for that thinking.

It is FAITH that makes a way for everyone. Only faith provides the key to that relationship and that paradise where we, one day, all meet together with the One who gave us the blessing of salvation, His Holy Spirit, and the fruits of the spirit that should remind us to thank Him always for His many benefits. Without this faith, this amazing faith, there would be no relationship.

It isn't always easy to understand yet it is the easiest thing to understand at the same time. Just believe. Those words, so short and sweet, mean more than all the words in the heart and soul. Just believe and find the peace that surpasseth all understanding. Just believe and receive the gift of salvation. Just believe and know the meaning of His grace and acceptance. Just believe and know the One who created every soul, every blessing, every faith. He gave us the faith and all we have to do is use that faith He provided to reach beyond this world with all it's materialism, into the spiritual world, where He provides the answers to every need, the beauty for every gesture, the miracles that bless the soul and bring freedom that restores all hope.

Just believe and know that, with Jesus, there is no reason to doubt because even in shadows, He inspires the love that divides dark from light. He is love and faith in Him will color the entire soul in hues of affection and hope. Just believe and never let go of

Day Twenty-One

the seed, the faith, God planted inside when you first agreed to follow Jesus, the One who saved your soul from the torment of an afterlife without God's precious light.

A Prayer and a Promise

Dear Lord, You know that I don't always have what it takes to make it through this world. I'm not always strong or brave or filled with the courage it takes to just let go of the fear and move forward. You fill my life, my soul, my faith, with belief that only You could have given me. Thanks to Your amazing love, Your sacrifice, Your gift to this world, I have the opportunity to become a child that You know inside. Thanks to You, dear Jesus, I know the love that brings me through the doubts, the clouds, the fears and tears, into the joy of a light that only Your beautiful love could have ignited. Thanks to You, my precious Savior, I know I don't have to work for salvation. This faith You gave me is the only thing I need. I love You and praise You. You simply amaze me!

> Any false religion ultimately is a deception of Satan, to try and keep people from the only way to Heaven, which is through faith in Jesus Christ.
> —Robert Jeffress

Day Twenty-Two

> Romans 5:1 Therefore being justified by faith, we have peace with God through our Lord Jesus Christ.

Being right with God or having peace with God is something that not everyone can claim. There are so many people in this world who don't know Jesus as their Lord and Savior. There are so many who believe being right with God or being justified by faith is simply going to church or giving, donating worldly goods or providing for missionaries.

While all of these gestures of love are certainly signs of faith, they don't—in their entirety—mean that someone is saved by faith. There are many who are deceived into believing that their works can save them and give them the key to heaven. There is nothing more mistaken than that way of thinking.

It is only faith in the One who lived, died and rose again—faith in Jesus Christ—that can assure our souls that we are free from sin, saved by grace, abiding in faith, remain in relationship with the King of Kings, and will, one day, be welcomed into the heavenly paradise where Jesus is living today.

It is so very simple. Believe and He sets you free. Believe and He gives you peace. Believe and know the One who brings about every dream, every grace, every breath. Believe and know what it is to have a new heart, a new life, a new hope. Believe and be set free from the sin that has destroyed so much of your life. Believe and know the joy that comes from being sanctified by Christ. Believe

Day Twenty-Two

and delight in the music that He plays for those who remember His sacrifice and give their hearts to following His light, His love, His path through this world.

There is no way I could explain the many ways that God has comforted me and reassured me that this faith in Him is a faith I will always be grateful for. Because of the faith that has taken me from darkness to light, from wrong to right, from sorrow to joy, from doubting to surety, I know that—with HIM, I can always be certain that whatever I do, so long as I follow His lead, I will be blessed in ways that I can't imagine with blessings that come in all shapes and forms.

Just a few days ago, one of these blessings (a material blessing though, most definitely, not all of the Lord's blessings are material blessings), came to me and my husband. We had been hoping to purchase a heater that was much too expensive for our budget. While we weren't sure where we'd get the money for the heater, we still set our hearts on getting one in the future. Because of my husband's allergies this heater would be even more of a blessing to us.

Due to unforeseen circumstances, an unexpected phone call and an even more surprised referral, we were—much sooner than we'd anticipated, able to purchase a heater that was exactly what we'd hoped for. And, the cost was so much lower than we'd expected that it was well within our budget. Actually, it was almost exactly what we would have hoped to spend if we'd written the cost down with our own pen, on our own terms, without a thought for the fact that we were probably dreaming because this price was absolutely too good to be true.

We got our heater, though, at a price we could easily afford. And, through the entire transaction, all I could think or say was that this, most assuredly, was God's doing, God's answer to prayer, God's kindness overflowing into blessings we'd never imagined. And, I am thankful, that even when I'm least expecting it, God shines His great light into my life and provides for me so beautifully that I could never thank Him enough with mere words.

PEARLS OF FAITH

A Prayer and a Promise

Dear Lord, Thank you for blessing me in more ways that I can possibly count. Your blessings truly are new each morning and they provide for me in ways I can't possibly explain. You are the wonderful counselor, the Prince of Peace, the King of Kings and I only pray that my faith in You will always remain a part of me. Because, precious Savior, I could never imagine my life without You in it. I could never be at peace if I was in a place where I didn't hear You speaking. No. I don't hear Your audible voice, but I do hear You speaking when things happen to me (like the heater purchase)—through loving hearts and tender moments, through the grace that pours out on me when I least expect it. Thank You, Jesus—You're my everything. There is no amount of praise that can do You justice. I love You!

> Of all the things Christ wants for us, loving Him and focusing our attention on Him are the most important.
> —Charles Stanley

Day Twenty-Three

> Acts 26:18 To open their eyes, and to turn them from darkness to light, and from the power of Satan unto God, that they may receive forgiveness of sins, and inheritance among them which are sanctified by faith that is in me.

My first book of Inspirational Christian Poetry was titled, A Light in the Darkness. Oh yes, Jesus is surely that light. He is the One who created light, both the morning sun and the moon who illuminates the night. He is also the One who sets hearts right and fills them with light. He is the light that provides peace and grace, hope and faith, love that will always amaze. He is the light that reaches beyond the darkest fears and gives hope to the doubting tears. He is the light who stills the winds, the storms, the rains, with peace that only He can give, peace that silences the fiercest dread. He is the light and He abides inside those who believe He is the One who came and died, then rose again, so that the entire world could have access to our Creator, a way out of the hell where Satan is waiting.

Paul, Jesus wonderous spirit who lived out his life following the LIGHT who abides inside those who believe He came to free the sinner and make a way for them to reach beyond this present darkness into the light of heaven where He is waiting to show them the home He has built there, the home meant to provide shelter and peace, the home that is a gift from the One who is stronger than any addiction, any crime, any reason we might find to ignore His call to follow where He leads, to give our greatest gift, our love, to the King of Kings. He saves us from the darkest doom and creates, inside us, a quiet assurance that wherever He may lead, so long as we follow Him, we'll be given the joy that our souls seek.

He opened Paul's eyes and gave him the gift of teaching, reaching others for the gospel, for hope, for faith, for grace, for the Jesus who made a way we'll always be thankful for. He let Paul know that, with Him, there is purpose and peace, promise and prayer, potential and praise. With Him, all things are possible and with Him, every good thing is actually probable.

I don't know the darkness that Paul knew. He was blind for days and had to be guided by someone, while he undoubtedly wondered if he would ever see the light of day again. He probably pondered on much more than is written down in the biblical account. He probably wondered what his future held, if he'd be blind forever, if he'd never be able to go back to the life he'd left when Jesus blinded him. Thankfully, he never would return to his old life. He'd move on to become a reflection of the One who designed him to be one of the chosen ones.

Even though he would see again very soon, Paul would not go back to the life he was living when Jesus blinded him. He would, indeed, be grateful for the Light that blinded him and find the joy that comes from knowing the One whose light is our ultimate peace. Because He met Jesus, He became one of God's greatest teachers, preachers, warriors for the Light who is Jesus Christ.

If we could only remember—when we find ourselves blinded by some sorrow or shadow, some doubt or despair, some fear or feeling—if we could only remember to simply praise our Maker, praise Him because He knows what it is we need and even though we don't want the struggles or discouragements, He knows what is best to help us grow into the souls He can use for the Kingdom that He's building, the Kingdom where we'll live eternally with the Light that is Him.

Day Twenty-Three

A Prayer and a Promise

Dear Lord, Please help me to remember to simply 'thank You' when I'm worried or fearful, when I'm struggling or desperate, when the darkness feels like it is closing in around my spirit and I am seeking the Light that is YOU more frantically than I've ever sought anything before. I want to thank You, Jesus, for those times when You're teaching me those things I need to learn in order to become the woman who You want me to be. Because of You, Jesus, I have grown into someone I would never have imagined I was capable of being and because of You and Your love, Your light, I know that this life is one that I bring as my sacrifice, hoping that it can bring fruit to Your kingdom, fruit that proves my first love is You, my King. Thank You, Jesus, for helping me to see the light when I try to fight the lessons that are there to make me better than I was before. Thank You, Lord, for You. You are the love that I can always be sure of and I'll always pray that I can do things YOUR WAY!

> God never made a promise that was too good to be true.
> —Dwight L. Moody

Day Twenty-Four

> Hebrews 12:2 Looking unto Jesus the author and finisher of our faith; who for the joy that was set before him endured the cross, despising the shame, and is set down at the right hand of the throne of God.

I wish I could tell you that I have a perfect understanding of the bible, but I do not and I'm quite sure that I won't ever have that perfect understanding—except, perhaps when I meet my Savior after I've left this life behind. And, like I can't understand everything the bible offers, I don't understand everything about the life that is to come. Therefore, even in the afterlife, I'm not sure what I'll understand and what I still will not understand. Only the Lord knows these things and only He can assure me that, despite my lack of knowledge, I will ultimately have a peace that is beyond understanding and a love that assures me my soul will forever be whole—in the presence of His all-consuming love.

There is an assurance that, whatever this life brings, through struggles and sorrows, temptations and trials, worries and doubts, I have One who knows everything I'm going through and He offers me the comfort of knowing, with Him,—although I am quite weak—I can make it through the worst that comes. With Him beside me, as a guide to me, I can overcome the trials with a promise of joy that I couldn't possibly imagine. Because He lives and because He gives my heart and soul the strength to face the challenges that would overwhelm me without Him beside me, I can be

Day Twenty-Four

certain that I have a faith, a sustaining faith, which will never let me down. This faith He gave me is the answer to so many struggles that I can't even begin to name them all.

When I feel like the darkness is spreading around my soul and I don't know the way out of the shadows, He silences the fears I have and restores me with love that is greater than any light I might have thought of. His light is a light that can ignite the most beautiful joys, the sweetest compassion and the wonders of love that knows no hesitation. With Him, there is love that gives and gives and gives, never stops giving. With Him, there is love that lives forever, silencing all the tears with comfort that could only come from the One who died and rose again to save me from a darkness that would mean I couldn't hope to find my way.

Letting go of every doubt, I listen to the still, small voice, the voice that gives me no choice except to love without conditions, to give without expectations, to devote myself to the One who silences every worry and reminds me that, with Him, I have faith that assures me when I'm down to my last chance. His is the hand I grasp when I feel like I'm being crushed by the weight of my past. His is the light I see when, everywhere—surrounding me, is a darkness that just won't leave. His is the answer to my every need and because of Him, I am sure. I believe!

He lived here on this earth. He knew the trouble we all face. He was tempted as we are tempted. Yet, He didn't ever sin. He was the perfect that we might yearn to be. He was the gentleness that whispers peace to the winds. He was the answer to all the doubts I hold within. Without this man named Jesus I wouldn't know what it means to live life with faith that allows me to breathe in the light and exhale the love. Without Him beside me I wouldn't know the meaning of faith that continues to believe, even through the worst grief. Because of Jesus, I am freer than I could ever hope to be and because of Jesus, I am sure of my destiny.

Pearls of Faith

A Prayer and a Promise

Dear Lord, Thank You for loving me! Thank You for coming to this world and providing each of us a way out of the muck and mire that seems to silence our greatest joy and frustrate our sweetest dreams. Because I know You, sweet Jesus, I know what it means to feel like everything really will be ok. I will be ok. Life, despite its sorrows, will be ok. You invite me to a faith that inspires me, excites me, invites me into a relationship that is more beautiful than I could have ever hoped for. Because of You, my Savior, I know what it is to love in ways that I couldn't have ever thought of. Thank You, Jesus. I love You!

> Through hard work, perseverance and a faith in God, you can live your dreams.
> —Ben Carson

Day Twenty-Five

Matthew 14:31 And immediately Jesus stretched forth his hand, and caught him, and said unto him, O thou of little faith, wherefore didst thou doubt?

I'm not sure if I still have it, but I had the T-shirt, the one that says "faith over fear". That seems to be what Jesus' question to Peter here is reminding. It takes faith over fear to see the miracles happen, to experience wonder of wonders, to know what it means to reach beyond normal into remarkable. It takes 'faith over fear' and I believe that is just what gave Peter the ability to take those first steps on the water. He believed in Jesus' miracle working power and he was able to walk on water. That is amazing, but Jesus asked him why he had doubted after this strong start of walking across the water. Why did he doubt?

It's doubt that silences our dreams. It's doubt that hushes our hope. It's doubt that quiets our faith. It's doubt that tempts us to just give up when we're so close to reaching out goal. Doubt is more than just hesitation. Doubt is the disbelief that keeps us on the reasoning side of those miracles that prove, beyond a doubt, that Jesus is just who He says He is. He is the king of kings, the Son of God, the Savior of our very souls. And, if we allow doubt to interfere with our faith in the Creator, His Son, the Holy Spirit who comforts when we hurt, we will be led into regret that we never wanted or expected.

It was doubt that discouraged Peter. And, it is doubt that will discourage us if we let it tempt us out of our faith in Jesus. Even when we feel uncertain or hesitant, there is a promise brought to life by the risen Savior. That promise is love beyond anything we could have ever imagined. His love can erase every doubt. It brings light to the darkness, embraces the sinner and allows the worst of us to see the way to a new life, a new hope, a new way—through Him, there is the promise that heaven awaits. All we need to do is tear down our doubts and listen to the faith that assures us He has made a way for us.

When Peter began to sink, it wasn't anything to do with Jesus' power. Jesus' power never lessened. He remained the all powerful, all loving, mighty Savior of the world—the Savior of Peter's soul. The thing that was different when Peter began to sink was Peter. He let doubt dissuade his believing. He let doubt cloud his thinking. He let doubt begin to sink him.

That is what we do, too. We often let doubt sink us. Even the most fervent believers, those who we can't imagine doubting at all, still experience their moments of weakness. It is during those weak moments, when doubt influences our faith and allows our passion for Christ to wan, that we feel our hearts and souls sinking beneath the muck and mire of the world's filth. We might fall into sin or we might simply refuse to hear Jesus when He is whispering in our ear. Whatever the case, if we doubt, we always find ourselves falling beneath the glow of His glorious light and our hearts, our souls, are never quite as beautiful as when they remain in that holy glow.

A Prayer and a Promise

Dear Lord, You know me better than I know me and I know that I have (just like Peter) struggled with doubt. When You told me to move and I was too afraid to, when You told me to give and I was greedy, when You told me to love and I was bitter—those times and so many others, I've let my doubts dim the glow that is Your love shining through to my soul. I hope that You know, despite my doubts, I know You're the only way through the clouds. You are

Day Twenty-Five

the only way I can find my way out of the sadness. You are the only way I know to find the answers meant for my soul. I love You, Jesus and I praise You with all that I am. I can only pray that the person I am brings reverence to You, my whole life's meaning. Thank You, Lord, for being the answer to every doubt I've ever experienced.

> The smallest seed of faith is better than the largest fruit of happiness.
> —Henry David Thoreau

Day Twenty-Six

Jesus loves you

Matthew 9:22 But Jesus turned him about, and when he saw her, he said, Daughter, be of good comfort; thy faith hath made thee whole. And the woman was made whole from that hour.

Jesus isn't just a man. He isn't just a teacher. He isn't just a preacher. He is God incarnate. He is the Prince of Peace. He is the King of Kings. He truly is EVERYTHING. And, throughout His life on earth, He responded to us, His people, with kindness, reassurance and so many miracles we're often overcome with wonder. His miracles—like turning water to wine, walking on the water as it flowed wildly beneath His feet, restoring the blind and, most importantly, forgiving the sins of those who sought redemption—His miracles so amazing, so dazing, our hearts should always be praising. He wasn't just any miracle worker. He was the greatest miracle worker ever known to us, mere mortals without the awesome power that was revealed through our great Savior.

One of Jesus' greatest miracles we know about was when the woman in the crowd had an issue of blood and she took it upon herself, believing in her heart that He could heal her, to touch the hem of His garment, sure that this would heal her. When she touched Him, immediately, Jesus felt what she'd done. He said power left Him and while He didn't ever chastise her for touching Him, He did ask who had touched Him. She came forward and He blessed her with the assurance that she'd certainly been healed and was now whole. She was blessed that day in ways that only God Himself could explain. It was truly a miracle that would forever be a part of God's word, His story, one of His greatest miracles.

While I've never touched Jesus' garment, I have touched Him with my prayers, my pleas, my yearnings, my hopes and my needs. He has worked miracles in me that I couldn't have ever imagined and the miracles that are most prominent for me are the ones that no one else on earth can see. They're the changes that have happened inside me. The changes from darkness to light, from wrong to right, from fearful to faithful, from worried to contented, from grieving to joyful, from disheartened to encouraged. Thanks to this man we call Jesus, I know what it means to be saved to the uttermost. With Him beside me, His spirit living inside me, I know what it means to love without expectations, to give selflessly, to live for someone other than myself, to live for the One who made me who I am and who continues to make me someone that not all people understand—someone who loves because of the love that He stirred up inside, love that lives beyond the grave, love that is His gift to those who have faith.

Faith might mean that some people will call me naïve or even stupid. Faith might mean that I sometimes do things others don't understand or recommend. Faith might mean that I give when I need or that I have strength when I'm at my weakest. Faith might mean that my heart breaks but I still plead for the peace of the one who hurt me. Faith might mean that I struggle with my greed, that I distance myself from darkness, that I feed the ones who stole from me. Faith might mean so many different things. But, most importantly, faith means that I can reach beyond the shadows that linger to discourage me and find the grace of that man named Jesus, who urges me to simply believe and continue to plant those seeds which might eventually grow into trees of faith who will someday grow seeds themselves.

A Prayer and a Promise

Dear Lord, Faith has brought me out of the desperation of my doubts, my distrust, my uncertainty, into a place filled with light and love, a place that I might have once imagined in my soul, but a place that I could never have expected to know without the faith YOU gave me. Thanks to the faith that You are who You say You are, I can always reach beyond this world and its pain, to the love and grace, the warmest faith, which teaches me that if I simply believe, I can always be sure that I'll win. Even when it doesn't look like I'm winning to someone else, as long as I have You, Jesus... I'm a winner. Even when I'm hurting, even when I'm worried, I know, deep inside, where you abide, that I have all I need to forever feel the joy and wonder of a love that I need never question. Your love, Jesus, is my life's greatest blessing. Thank You, Love. You're my most cherished possession!

> Faith is the strength by which a shattered world shall emerge into the light.
> —Helen Keller

Day Twenty-Seven

Revelation 1:5 And from Jesus Christ, who is the faithful witness, and the first begotten of the dead, and the prince of the kings of the earth. Unto him that loved us, and washed us from our sins in his own blood,

Blood is gross. It means pain, hurt, injury. It means feeling sick, distressed, poorly. And, even when it is taken by a qualified nurse or caregiver, it is a bit nauseating for me. I don't like blood. And, when the preacher preaches on the importance of the blood being applied to my life, I get a little skittish. Blood has that effect on me. It isn't that I doubt the importance of Jesus' blood being applied to me. It's that I just wish it was something less upsetting, less gross. Something like milk or honey, the things talked about in the Old Testament when the Israelites were headed to their promised land.

It isn't milk or honey that can wash me white as snow, though. And, despite my queasy stomach, it will never be anything less than the blood of Christ that will make me into someone worthwhile, someone who is promised a place in heaven, someone who can stand before God without expecting obliteration because when someone like me, a sinner who has sinned unsparingly, faces a Holy God, there is little doubt that I'm about to face judgement and ruin—without that blood which means He only sees the innocence of His beloved Son, Jesus, the One and Only Savior of the world. Even though blood is gross, the blood of Jesus is something that cleanses my whole heart, my whole soul, my whole life, making it possible for me (the sinner that is in so much need) to come face to face with the One who created me.

If I think of it that way, reflecting on the assurance of grace that sustains, the faith that saves, the wonder of this blood that cleans every stain, erasing—not just my sin, but even the sin that I've committed again and again, the sin that seems to follow me all my life, leaving its mark upon my spirit and its deafening screams upon my best intentions of following after the One who made a way for me to be saved—I don't feel so woozy because it is the red stuff that flows through our veins. When I remember what He came to give us, the wonder of eternal life with Him, I won't allow that unsettled feeling to conquer my feelings. It is this blood that cleanses me. It is this blood that frees me. It is this blood that gives me the victory.

When I remember that this blood, this divine blood that erases even the least sign of a future in hell or a life without the peace that He gives, I am so very grateful that He came to earth, lived and died and rose again so that this blood of His could cleanse me in a way that no earthly blood, water or any liquid possibly could. This blood He washes those who believe in Him in, is the blood that silences every doubt, reassures every prayer, invites those who love Him to become more like Him as they follow Him into the most beautiful eternity.

The thought of blood can make me queasy. But the thought of His love, revealed through His blood, washing away my sins, making me whole again—this is enough to remind me that this blood, His blood, is my hope for everlasting joy and peace, love that silences all of my grief, the promise of life because I surely do believe—His blood has washed me clean!

A Prayer and a Promise

Dear Lord, You already know that blood can gross me out—but, You also know, that I love YOU without any doubt and I believe that Your blood bathed me in a love that is more beautiful than

Day Twenty-Seven

any love I will ever be able to explain. It is Your blood, Your love, that gives me a reason to shine with the light that You gave to me when You saved me. This light is the light that glistens in my eyes, invites hearts to see what You have done—because You came to save me even though I thought I wanted to be alone. Now that You have forgiven me, saved me and cleansed me with Your own blood, I know what it means to feel like I'm the richest woman on earth, the most blessed, the most fortunate. Because of You, Jesus, and the blood that washed my soul, I know what it means to breath easy because I don't have any reason to fear death or the life that comes next, the life that will surely be more amazing than I can guess. Thank You, Lord, for the blood that washed me clean so I can come before God knowing that He sees Your innocence instead of my iniquity.

> The blood was shed to unite us to God.
> —Andrew Murray, The Power Of The Blood Of Jesus

Day Twenty-Eight

> Romans 12:3 For I say, through the grace given unto me, to every man that is among you, not to think of himself more highly than he ought to think; but to think soberly, according as God hath dealt to every man the measure of faith.

I have my doubts. No. I don't doubt that God saved my soul—at least not most of the time. I've even doubted my salvation at times. Especially when I fail Him and that happens all to often. But, in spite of my doubts, I keep pushing on. I keep clinging to Him and—though trembling at times, (with fear and trembling), I move my feet forward, trudging on and on, hoping that I'm making my way to the places, to the people, to the light where He can use me. Yes. I want Him to use me even though I'm underqualified, unsuitable and unworthy. Despite all of those facts about myself, I want Him to use me. I pray that He will use me and I'm sure that, if He does use me, it will certainly be because He can use even the least among us. If He uses me at all, I pray that His amazing spirit will bring me through the darkness into His grace, His love, His light—the melody of a beautiful so abundant it stirs even the worst of us to give a piece of us even though we can never be enough.

I have my doubts. I don't believe I'm useful. I don't believe I'm worthy. I don't believe I have what it takes to lead another heart to the destiny that I'm still working out (with fear and trembling)

Day Twenty-Eight

myself. I have my doubts, but He has my back. He makes a way where I can't see a way. He silences my fears and erases my despair. He fills me with His courage, His peace, His grace. He makes me believe that I can when I am still thinking I can't.

I have my doubts. Yes. I have my doubts that I can do anything that might be good for the King of Kings, the Savior of my soul, the reason that I believe and so very much more. I have my doubts. But, I believe and because I believe, I know that there is a light far brighter than any of my clouds. There is a Son far wiser than any knowledge I possess. There is a love far more abundant than any shame I might have felt. Because He lives, I can silence those doubts that come to me—because I am absolutely correct. In and of myself, I can do absolutely nothing. My doubts are not without merit. I cannot. I don't have it in me. Yet, I do have it in me because I have the Holy Spirit living within me.

His Holy Spirit is leading me through the worst darkness I face. He is guiding me when I can't see past the shadows that are haunting me. He is wise and clever and He helps me to listen to that still, small voice, the same One that silenced my heart when it attempted to break beyond repair. That same love that saved me gave me the ability to understand that when He says I can it doesn't really matter what I think. All my doubting is nothing at all to Him because when He says I can, there is only one way through the doubt and that is through Him. When I listen to the voice of love and remember that it comes from the One who overcame this world, I know that I can do anything He directs me to do.

I have my doubts. But, He has a certainty that will overcome whatever doubt might be troubling me. He knows when I don't know. He promises I can go where He leads. He is my hope, my assurance, my security. With Him beside me, guiding me, I can face anything that comes into my life with the assurance that—because of Him and His love—I really am enough.

Pearls of Faith

A Prayer and a Promise

Dear Lord, Thank You for challenging me and for leading me to victory in so many situations that I couldn't possibly name them all. You have shown me that, despite my doubts, I can rely on Your light to shine so that I can see beyond that darkness that tries to swallow me up and leave me in the dark. I can see that, because I believe in You, I have all I need to make it through whatever comes. Thank You, Jesus, for helping me to see the light. You are the wonder of wonders. You are the hope that silences my heart when it beats with fear. You are the grace that stirs my soul to never let go of Your hand. You are the reason that I never will know what it means to be lonely again. I love You, Lord, more than anything.

> Faith is unseen but felt, faith is strength when we feel we have none, faith is hope when all seems lost.
> —Catherine Pulsifer

Day Twenty-Nine

Galatians 2:20 I am crucified with Christ: nevertheless I live; yet not I, but Christ liveth in me: and the life which I now live in the flesh I live by the faith of the Son of God, who loved me, and gave himself for me.

My Jesus loving Mom once bought me a sweatshirt that, on the front, read, "It's not about me!" On the back was one word. JESUS.

This statement is so true that I can't say it enough. It's not about me! It is absolutely NOT about me! It's about Him, the Son of God, the King of Kings, the Prince of Peace, the Lord, the Lamb, the great I AM. It is all about Him. Jesus is the reason for every season. Jesus is the answer to every prayer prayed. Jesus is the joy that kindles hope inside the believer. Jesus is the whisper of light that rests on those who can't find the way through the darkness. Jesus is my meaning, my serenity, my wisdom. He is the way through every storm and He is the hope that will keep a heart warm. He is love and He lives above, where we'll be going so long as we know HIM.

One of my first memories is being in a old timey country church, singing Jesus Loves Me to the top of my lungs and knowing that, even though I wasn't always the good little girl Mama hoped for, I was someone that the King of Kings had died for. And, because I know that love that only He could have provided, I know that I'm saved from the darkness and the fire, a hell where His

Spirit would not accompany, where my soul would never know the beauty of His grace, the joy in His face, the wonder of His embrace.

That long ago memory of singing Jesus Loves Me is just as appropriate now that I'm 58 years old and entering the autumn of my journey here on earth. Jesus LOVES me and I can trust in the love forever and ever. Without a doubt, He has always been with me and He will stay with me throughout time and into the eternal where His light will shine so that I can see through my worst into the miracle of a life that will never end, a life with my very best friend. Because I know Him, because my hope is in Him, because His love brings me peace within, there is not one single doubt that I'll escape the despair of hell where those who reject Him will someday find themselves. Because HE IS THE ANSWER I can always be assured of the direction I'm headed when this life has ended.

But, even though He gave me eternity to praise Him, IT'S NOT ABOUT ME! It's all about Jesus, and the more I turn my hope toward Him, the more I silence the selfishness within, the more I realize His Spirit will carry me through to the end, the more I can turn my heart from my own fears, my own tears, toward the beauty of living for the One who died and rose so that I would someday reap the benefits of His love. His benefits remind me, more often than not, that I am so unworthy, but because HE IS WORTHY, I will serve Him as if my life depended on it. And, it does. My life depends on the One who saved me from sin that meant to keep me in the dark throughout my life and eternity. Because He is my best friend, because I believe in HIM, I have complete peace within. I know, because of Him, I can enter eternity without dread. Because I believe, I've been redeemed.

A Prayer and a Promise

Dear Lord, You always remind me that You're 100% behind me. You make a way where I can see only closed doors. You give me light when I am in the dark. You stir my heart when I feel so lost. You lift my soul when it is downtrodden. You are the One who

Day Twenty-Nine

assures me of hope that will forever bring me through the storms of this life, and into an eternity where Your love will abide throughout all time. I can never praise You enough for the miracle of Your love, Your kindness, Your grace and mercy and peace. I love You, Jesus and I know that You love me. That is enough to reassure me throughout life and on, through the passage into eternity where I'll finally meet you face to face and feel the passion of Your unending grace. Thank You, Jesus. I can't wait to meet You—even though I already know You!!

> I am trying here to prevent anyone saying the really foolish thing that people often say about Him: I'm ready to accept Jesus as a great moral teacher, but I don't accept his claim to be God. That is the one thing we must not say. A man who was merely a man and said the sort of things Jesus said would not be a great moral teacher. He would either be a lunatic—on the level with the man who says he is a poached egg—or else he would be the Devil of Hell. You must make your choice. Either this man was, and is, the Son of God, or else a madman or something worse. You can shut him up for a fool, you can spit at him and kill him as a demon or you can fall at his feet and call him Lord and God, but let us not come with any patronizing nonsense about his being a great human teacher. He has not left that open to us. He did not intend to.
> —C.S. Lewis, Mere Christianity

Day Thirty

2 Timothy 3:15 And that from a child thou hast known the holy scriptures, which are able to make thee wise unto salvation through faith which is in Christ Jesus.

I met a woman I'll call Izzy. She is a firm believer in Jesus and she has always gone to a Pentecostal church where they frequently speak in tongues. I go to a Baptist church where they frequently praise and worship, but don't have any members who speak in tongues. At least, not to my knowledge.

As someone who has gone to a Pentecostal church and heard followers speaking in tongues, I don't doubt that this gift is something that is valid for some believers. I believe in speaking in tongues. What I don't believe is that speaking in tongues is a requirement of salvation. My friend, Izzy, does believe that speaking in tongues is a requirement of salvation. Izzy thinks that those who don't speak in tongues don't have the indwelling of the Holy Spirit. Needless to say, I believe I have the Holy Ghost living inside me and I haven't been able to speak in tongues. So, Izzy and I disagree about the requirements of salvation.

When I spoke to Izzy about my beliefs she became somewhat defensive and left me with only one recourse, to shut my mouth! I tried to tell her what I believed. I looked up my reasons for my belief, which assures me that I am saved and, yes, I do have the Holy Spirit, even though I've failed to meet Izzy's requirement which is to speak in tongues. I googled the questions on speaking

Day Thirty

in tongues and gave Izzy a website to visit which confirmed (with scripture references) my belief. Izzy came back the following day and told me she didn't have any questions, but, quite obviously, was put off by my pursuit of answers. So, I SHUT MY MOUTH.

I don't know how to argue with someone like Izzy. She is so sure of her belief that speaking in tongues is a requirement of salvation, that she ignores any possibility that people can be saved without this gift being given to them.

Because I have been to a Pentecostal church and have struggled with the hope of speaking in tongues and known the disappointment of not being blessed with that gift, I know that Izzy is totally sincere in her beliefs. She is not trying to be confrontational. She just believes what she believes and I struggle with understanding her close minded attitude. I struggle to understand why she doesn't understand that not every gift of the spirit is given to every believer. Yes. There was Pentecost and the believers there were given that beautiful gift from heaven. But there are so many other believers who haven't been blessed in that way. Just as sincerely as Izzy believes that those who don't speak in tongues are headed for hell, I believe that those believers—because of grace, through faith—are headed to heaven.

Finally, I have prayed for Izzy—though not in tongues because I don't know how to speak in tongues. Perhaps she has prayed for me in tongues. Either way, I believe the Lord hears and I believe it is up to Him and only Him who He blesses with which gifts of the spirit He decides to.

Unlike Izzy, who thinks I am on my way to hell because I don't speak in tongues, I believe that she is headed to heaven, simply because of her faith. We disagree on some things, but, needless to say, God is checking our hearts—not our head knowledge—and only He has the power to forgive and that forgiveness is surely the answer that leads us into His presence. Like the thief on the cross, who didn't have time to speak in tongues or do anything but believe, I am counting on my faith, my believing, to take me through this life and into the next where I believe I'll be with the One who forgave me and saved me!

Pearls of Faith

A Prayer and a Promise

Dear Lord, I love You and I pray—even though I don't pray in tongues—that You will read through my head knowledge and see into my heart where I am sure You've provided me with the Holy Spirit, the Comforter, the One who helps me through this life and who I will forever be grateful for. Because I know You, Jesus, are the light of my world, I am praising and praying that You will lead me to those words You want me to say. Help me to share YOU with others and glorify Your name with every step I take. I love You, Lord and will forever be grateful for the faith that You sustain!

> Faith is unseen but felt, faith is strength when we feel we have none, faith is hope when all seems lost.
> —Catherine Pulsifer

Day Thirty-One

Jesus loves you

Acts 16:5 And so were the churches established in the faith, and increased in number daily.

I'm a member of a Pentecostal church where I attended church nearly three decades ago. I haven't ever changed my membership from that church to the church I currently go to, which is a Missionary Baptist church. And, I've never felt like I was sinning or wrong or failing the Lord in some way by my attendance in either church. Actually, both of these churches brought me closer to Jesus and more infallible in my understanding of scriptures, spirituality and the promises of God. Each of these amazing churches served to minister to my soul in ways that I can't even begin to describe and I'm grateful for my experience with both places.

Since I've gone to the Pentecostal church, I've met believers who attempted to persuade me into believing that speaking in tongues is a requirement of salvation. Despite what others might believe, I don't believe this principle. I've already written a devotional on an incident I've had with a friend who I once confronted on this subject. And, unless the Lord convinces me otherwise, I can't imagine how speaking in tongues could be necessary for my salvation. Even though I believe this gift is a wonderful endowment from the spirit and one that I would like to have myself, I don't believe it is essential to salvation. What I do believe is that (Ephesians 2:8) For by grace are ye saved through faith; and that not of yourselves: it is the gift of God: And, I also believe that when someone tries to draw lines between the different churches who believe in Jesus and believe in the grace that saves, they are mistaken.

In Acts 16:5, Paul was explaining to the new Christians that these new believers, mostly Gentiles, didn't need to be circumcised to be saved. Even though some of the Jewish believers maintained that believers needed to be circumcised, Paul told them that they were saved—even though they weren't circumcised. It seems to be the same in ways today as it was way back when—as some churches take their traditions more seriously than their faith or the grace that brought them into the presence of One who made a way out of their pain, their doubts, their sins—into the love that only God could have given them.

This is a love that makes the foolish wise and the dead in sin—He brings back to life. With Him bringing salvation to the soul, there is the wonder of a new birth, a new life, a new hope. And, this hope is more powerful than any hope we've ever known. This hope will bring us into the very heaven that some of us may never have even heard of before we met Him, the heaven where Jesus sits on the right hand of the Father, making intercession for those of us who have sought Him and discovered the grace that saves despite the darkness of our hearts and the wrongs that make us sure we are the worst of the worst. We deserve death and hell, but because He forgives, we have the chance to escape those things because God Himself casts our sin so far away that He will never have to see those sins again.

Even if we think of those sins in our past and remember the way we were before He brought us into the light that healed us, there is no reason to feel ashamed anymore. Our mess (our past) is, as they say. . . our message. His forgiveness changed our destiny. We're not on our way to death and hell, but instead we're on

Day Thirty-One

a journey of love that only He could have spoken into us. Because of Jesus, we have the hope of forever and because of Jesus and the faith that He stirred inside, we know the joy that comes to those who are blessed throughout all time.

A Prayer and a Promise

Dear Lord, Because I'll be with You forever in heaven, I know that I have the chance to understand, then, more than I do today. When the time comes and I am by Your side, I believe there will be answers for all the things that are obscured now. I'll know why speaking in tongues is a gift I haven't been given, yet a gift that some were blessed with. I'll know how the churches I've attended have shed light on my understanding and brought me closer to You. I'll know more than I know now and most importantly, I'll be with YOU forever, praising the way that only the forgiven can praise—with a heart that is grateful to know the power of Your NAME. I love You, Jesus and am so excited for the moment when I meet you face to face. With all my heart, I'm grateful beyond what my heart can explain.

> Faith is not the belief that God will do what you want. It is the belief that God will do what is right.
> —Max Lucado, He Still Moves Stones: Everyone Needs a Miracle

Day Thirty-Two

1 Thessalonians 5:8 But let us, who are of the day, be sober, putting on the breastplate of faith and love; and for an helmet, the hope of salvation.

It was love that erased our sin debt. It was love that silenced the old man. It was love that destroyed the fear we felt. It was love that lifted the darkness left by the pain and doubt. It was love that broke through our hard hearts and left a gentle, a meek, a faint assurance that whatever is to come—be it sorrows or hurts, wonders or warmth, laughter or tears, whatever is to be, there is that amazing love brought to life in us who believe. Faith, it seems, has brought to life something more amazing than we could have ever dreamt. This love, this hope, this faith is the answer to our every need. These three fill our hearts, create an intimacy with the One who created us and everything, abides because what we've learned is that, with God, all things truly are possible.

There was a time when my faith fell apart. I was a mess inside. Anxiety and panic shuddered in the depths of my spirt. On the outside I was the same woman I'd always been, while inside, I was shattered by my encounters with my own doubts and sin. My faith was buried somewhere, in a place I couldn't disclose. While my mind was leaving shadows across my thoughts, breaking away each sound thought and replacing them with irrational feelings, dark dread and fear, nervousness that was like an unending apprehension, a feeling that couldn't even breath for the lack of air, that

Day Thirty-Two

sustaining air that comes from believing. Faith, it felt, had decided to pull up roots and leave me to the wolves of doubt and despair. It felt like everywhere I turned, each blessing had been submerged in uncertainty and suspicion. I was paranoid and desperate, filled with misgivings and distrust. I ached for the feeling that comes from knowing, just knowing—with faith that assures and sustains. But, wherever I turned, I could only catch glimpses of panic.

This time, my time of fright, flustered and alone, was the place I finally came to know that—when in the dark, there comes a SON whose light is brighter than the morning, whose promises are more precious than the greatest riches, whose assurance of grace, whose blessings of faith, quiet every anxiety, replacing those fears that eat away the soul with guarantee that Jesus is the answer to every anxiety. Just as I'd given up on the peace that comes from knowing, from believing, from agreeing with the faith that prepares hearts for love that never grows old, He reached down with His promise to secure me with His love and reassured me that whatever I might face, wherever I go—to the heavens above or the darkest of sorrows—He is right there beside me, reminding me that faith in Him, in His promises, will uphold me during the worst there is. Because of Jesus, I know that I can face anything life throws at me with faith that, because He is, because He lives, I have a better home waiting in the eternal.

Salvation! That is the blessed assurance that replaced my fear, my worry and anxiety, with a peace that comes to hearts who know this man who came to us in the form of a baby, died on a cross and rose again, blessing all believers with the promise of everlasting life. This man is Jesus Christ and His sacrifice took away all my sins, all my fears, replacing them with peace that sustains me even when the darkest moments cause me to tremble within. The faith I have in Him is faith that only God could have stirred inside my soul. It is a faith that guides me through the doubts and sorrows and assures me that I'll always know the joy that comes to life inside those who know His only Son as the One who cancelled the debt owed and replaced that debt with an appointment to meet with the King of Kings and accept the key to a heavenly home.

Pearls of Faith

A Prayer and a Promise

Dear Lord, You know how deeply this faith You placed inside my heart goes. You know that, because You live, I live—because You died, I die to self—because You were gentle and kind, because You restored my mind when I felt like I was without a hope, because You are the light that shines faith through my soul—I know that I'll never let go of the promise You brought to me through Your precious words. I know that because I believe in You, the One who is guiding me through faith that secures my hope, my love, my peace, I have everything I will ever need. Jesus, YOU ARE MY EVERYTHING. Thank You for bringing me through the sorrow, the pain, the anxiety. Thank You for inviting me into a relationship with the King of Kings. Thanks to You, Jesus, I truly am living my soul's dream! I love You.

> We can't solve modern problems by going back in time. Retreating to the safety of the familiar is an understandable response, but God has called us to a life of faith. And faith requires us to face the unknown while trusting Him completely.
> —Charles R. Swindoll

Day Thirty-Three

> Galatians 3:22 But the scripture hath concluded all under sin, that the promise by faith of Jesus Christ might be given to them that believe.

No one can keep the laws God gave to those who lived before Jesus was brought back to life, the living sacrifice for sin, the One who lived, died and rose again so that we could all know the meaning of a love that is a gift beyond our comprehension. God's love is beyond understanding and the faith that He provided to those who seek the light of His grace, His love, His salvation, is a faith that saves from the worst of all possible endings—the end that means eternity without Him.

Without His presence, we are assuredly doomed to outer darkness, to a hell that only the worst of the worst, the devil and his demons, was meant for. People were not meant for hell. We were not meant for the fire that is never quenched, the darkness that is never eased, the pain and the agony that will never cease. But because people have chosen, of their own free will, to let go of the God who reigns, to seek out the darkness of that dreaded place, there are people in hell today. And, even if they didn't believe in Jesus when they were here on earth, I know that they assuredly believe today and would definitely give anything to have a second chance to pray the sinner's prayer and get saved from that awful place.

While here, we still have the opportunity to reach out to Jesus, to seek the light that is His love, to believe in the One God sent to accept us into His body, His church. Through the faith that He gave us, we can find redemption from the darkness that abides in those who don't know Him as Savior and King, as the One who made the world and the One who died and rose again so we could be saved from that worst of possible endings.

I went into a bar just this past weekend. No. I didn't know how that would feel when I entered the doors and I wasn't there for a drink after work the way so many of the other patrons were. Instead, I'd had the pizza they make recommended to me by a coworker. I called in my order and went in to pick it up. Once upon a time, I'd had my share of wine and beer, but when I stood at the bar waiting for my order, I looked around the dimly lit room and realized that I'd lived—yes, lived in sin—but also, I'd lived for myself in a way that I can sincerely say makes me feel sick to think of today. I was lost. I was without hope. I was in the darkness that causes hearts to grow cold.

Thank God, now, today... I know Him in a way that has taken away the darkness from my soul. I can honestly say that I love Jesus more than I ever loved the past woman who lived so selfishly and so errantly. Because of the One who made a way for me, the One who I've placed all my faith in, I know that there is a place where I'll spend eternity with the very One who created me, the One who intercedes for me, the One who saved me to the uttermost and the One who I'll spend forever praising, worshipping, honoring. Not only do I love Jesus more than I can say. I also love the way He's changed me from dark to light, from sad to glad, from fearful to faithful. Because of Jesus, I know that I'm saved from the law's condemnation, and, from the hell where so many will spend forever. Because of the faith He gave, the faith He sustains, I know that He has made a way for believers to avoid that destiny meant for the devil and his angels.

A Prayer and a Promise

Dear Lord, You know me better than I know myself. You have changed me from the sinner doomed to hell to the saint who is

Day Thirty-Three

preparing for heaven. You changed me from darkness to light, from fearful to fearless, from weary to robust. You changed me from the failure I once was to the hopeful I have become. You changed me from weak and alone, to someone who is strengthened by Your love. Thanks to You, dear Lord, I know what it means to be saved from sin, saved from fear, saved from shame, saved from the past that haunts my spirit, saved from the hell that I'll never see, saved from the doubts that plague the sinner. Thank You, Jesus, for saving me! I love You.

Put your nose into the Bible everyday. It is your spiritual food. And then share it. Make a vow not to be a lukewarm Christian.
—Kirk Cameron

Day Thirty-Four

Mark 5:34 And he said unto her, Daughter, thy faith hath made thee whole; go in peace, and be whole of thy plague.

One small word holds the key to all life, all hope, all eternity. It is this simple word that can make hearts whole, still the doubts and fears, destroy the worst of our anxieties and leave us—not only better, but at peace with the One who created us to be in a relationship with Him. One small word and that word is faith.

Faith makes a way where there is no way. Faith quiets the demons that taunt us with their endless temptations and invitations. Faith reminds us that we're the children of One who can cure any pain, dry every tear, treat any illness and heal anything that might cause us even a shadow of doubt. Faith is the answer to our prayers and the reason we pray. Faith is the clearest sign that we are the children of One who lets us live our lives in freedom, with free will, while quietly reminding us that we are meant to, above all else, have faith in the One who came down to us from heaven and taught us about the love that is more amazing than any love we'll ever experience on this earth.

Jesus told the woman with the issue of blood that her FAITH had made her whole. He didn't say her kindness made her whole. He didn't say her goodness made her whole. He didn't say her giving made her whole. No. He said her FAITH had made her whole!

Day Thirty-Four

Faith changes things. When we use faith in our prayers, changes are sure to come. When we use faith in our everyday lives, changes are promised. When we use faith in our hearts and souls, changes are assured. Faith changes hearts and souls, lives and goals, hopes and dreams. It isn't kindness, goodness or giving that inspires change so much as the faith it takes to do the good things in a way that only faith can enthuse. Faith is the answer to even the boldest questions. Faith is an anchor in this sea of brokenness that reminds us we're connected to the One who tells the sun when to rise and leaves a trail of stars across the night's skies.

When we don't know what to do there is one thing that remains true. Faith can change even the worst that has come. Faith changes things and sustains hearts in ways that can't be explained. Faith is the answer to every fear, each pain, every reason we might have to doubt. Faith, even the smallest faith, can take us from the darkness to the light, from the shame to honorable, from the weak to the strong. Faith can decide our fate and faith in the One who chose us to love can lead us on the path that will assure us of a home in heaven when we move out of this world into the eternal world.

On those days when I don't feel like I have the faith I need to make it through those places of darkness and despair, I do something that only faith could allow me to do. I pray and I pray to One who can increase my faith so that I have what it takes to move beyond the darkness into the light of His love.

A Prayer and a Promise

Dear Lord, On those days when my faith is weak, please lift my spirit with the light, the love, the faith that only You could give me. Please restore in me a faith that makes me whole, a faith that embraces hearts, a faith that takes away the doubts. Please answer my prayers with the reminder that, with faith—in YOU,—all things are possible. I have my fears. I have my doubts. I have my needs and I have my sorrows. But, because of YOU, dear Jesus, I have somewhere to turn with every problem, every fear, every tear. Because of YOU, Jesus, I have a faith that reassures me there is always a new hope, a new light, a new grace. Because of You and this faith that You gave me—I am saved. Thank You, Lord. I love You and am so amazed by You.

> Christian faith is . . . basically about love and being loved and reconciliation. These things are so important, they're foundational and they can transform individuals, families.
> —Philip Yancey

Day Thirty-Five

1 Timothy 4:1 Now the Spirit speaketh expressly, that in the latter times some shall depart from the faith, giving heed to seducing spirits, and doctrines of devils;

A few days ago I saw a post on a social networking site, and it reminded me that there are so many questionable practices going on in our world. The post specifically mentioned the demonic activity surrounding things like horoscopes, numerology, psychics, the use of sage and so much more. These are the more obvious 'seducing spirits' that Paul reminds us of in the previous verse. Other, less obvious false doctrines, might be preachers who seem to encourage abortions, same sex encounters and even same sex marriages, and many other obvious rejections of clear, biblical doctrine.

I don't ever want to encourage anyone to believe something which is recognizably against the One we serve as practicing Christians. I hope that I will always be able to turn believers away from the demonic or satanic. I never want to risk my own faith by supporting a practice that is most assuredly evil in the sight of the God we serve, the God who is love, the God who is doubtless more than a little angry when His children are enticed by the very demonic spirits that He cast out of His home in heaven all those decades ago.

When Paul mentions these seducing spirits he is reminding all of us to search our hearts, our souls, our lives, for the inklings of dark habits, dark thoughts, dark natures that cleverly silence our need to obey the One who gave up heaven to come to earth and be the sacrifice for us who could never have been good enough to enter heaven where God abides forever and ever. Because He lived, died and came back to us after three days in the tomb, we can be certain that whatever happens in this life—through pains, sorrows and tears—there is always a light waiting up ahead, casting its beauty all through our hearts, remembering that it is love Jesus taught. But, also, He taught us to avoid the darkness that dims our light and even colors hope distraught.

I love Jesus more than words can say. Even when I praise with poetry and song, through day and night, through my life and my light—there is a yearning that reminds me, throughout this life and into eternity, despite all my spirit's praising, I can never begin to arrive at the amazing that Jesus provided to each heart who hears His call and welcomes Him so that they're forever His. Nothing and no one can ever bring satisfaction the way that Jesus' love will. His love is the answer to every tear, each fear, the many years of anxiousness that reveal to us the need for a Savior who is forever giving—forever living, forever forgiving. He is our light, our heart, our prayer and our promise. He is our hope, our need, our life and our reason. He is the answer to every doubt. He leads us out of the shadows and into the spirit's breathless gentleness. He is light. He is love. He is alive and He lives in us!

Without this Jesus who saved my soul, there is no way I would ever know what it means to love without an agenda, to give without expectations, to live for someone other than myself, to live for One who made the world and every soul who lives. Without this Jesus who created the heart, the soul, the music that rings throughout eternity, I would never know the joy of sensitivity, tranquility, serenity. I would never know the beauty that comes to those who believe without proof, the One who silenced every doubt when He came out of that tomb!

Day Thirty-Five

A Prayer and a Promise

Dear Lord, There is a darkness that can destroy the light, a darkness that can silence the praise, a darkness that can leave doubt in its wake. I don't want to go through the darkness but know that sometimes I will encounter that darkness because I'm living in a world that is edged in it, a world that confesses it, a world that is lost in its black. I live in a world that I hope to change by bringing the light of Your love wherever I walk, the light of Your hope wherever I smile, the light of Your grace in whatever I face. I hope that, when I give them JESUS, I give them the answer to this darkness that the whole world is so absorbed by. I hope, dear Lord, that—because of You—I can be a light in the darkness and a reminder that, through grace, through faith, through Jesus Christ, the living hope—there is a chance to emerge from the dark with a glow that reminds us all, love is alive and He abides inside those who believe in Jesus, the way, the truth, the life. Thank You, Lord, for giving us the chance to know You and grow to be the Christians that You knew we could be when You gave up Your life on earth to change the whole world.

> The more I am in a position to be tried in faith with reference to my body, my family, my service for the Lord, my business, etc., the more shall I have opportunity of seeing God's help and deliverance; and every fresh instance, in which He helps and delivers me, will tend towards the increase of my faith.
> —George Muller

Day Thirty-Six

Jesus loves you

2 Corinthians 4:13 We having the same spirit of faith, according as it is written, I believed, and therefore have I spoken; we also believe, and therefore speak;

When I'm met with some encounter that causes me frustration, later on I usually think of some bible verse or meditation that I might have quoted or declared to provide the frustrater with an argument that couldn't have reasonably been countered. This was the case when I visited my local grocery store a few days ago.

I met a woman who I'd known many years ago, a woman who spoke kind words but also spoke of so much 'trash' meant to discredit the Holy words of God. She is, no doubt, on the road to a place that I won't ever see, a place of darkness and desperation, a place I would like to see her saved from. But, on that road, she seems determined to travel, walking all the more quickly when met with the words that Jesus gave me to dispute her dark discouragements.

She is someone that I have thought of often because her persona is so evil. Evil is a strong word, but one I use with the utmost caution. When I think of her, I think of witchcraft, wickedness, the

Day Thirty-Six

darkest of hearts. I believe she intends, with all her might, to destroy the very things that live inside God's chosen hearts. She comes to believers with the deafening tests of faith that could only be called exasperating. She is a strong force of darkness but I have no doubt that the Jesus I serve as Master is stronger, wiser and more vigilant in pursuing souls than the worst of our adversary's servants.

Although I would like to destroy the doubt she secretes in her every word, I have no way of forcing my faith on her or anyone who travels the road of evil. She is lost and I can't save her. I can, however, plant seeds. I can tell her what I believe—that Jesus is my Lord and Savior, that Jesus is the light who can save her, that Jesus is the heart's Redeemer and through Jesus—there is a way out of the darkness, through the despair, into the light where even the shadows seem brighter. If she listens to one word I speak, there isn't a doubt in me that it is the words Jesus place in my heart, words of faith, words of grace, words meant to present her with truth that will never fade... these are the words, the seeds planted by a love that only He could have brought forth from my soul, that are capable of changing the worst of the worst, changing the evil soul to one who is good, changing the doubting heart to a believer who may be someone who changes the world.

It is only through faith that He poured out inside me that I'm able to whisper hope through my pores, oozing light through my insights, emitting love that only God Himself could have placed in me (YES! It is HIM, not I)—a heart who believes but a heart who knows, without a doubt, that He is the reason for every joy, every smile, every grace that finds a way to reveal the love that He placed inside my soul. Because He lives, I have a reason to silence the doubts that sometimes silence my dreams and reach beyond this present sorrow, into the glistening faith that sheds light on every dream. His love erases the melancholy, the despair, the faded echoes of that woman I met—the one who terrorizes with her words of doubt, the one who tells me my faith is a lie, the one who speaks distrust into my life, the one who reminds me, with her lies, of the reasons I have for believing, beyond any doubt, that God sent us His Son to die and come back to life, so that I would know love more beautiful than anything this world might offer, beautiful love that is beyond words or description, a wonderful that is because Jesus forgives.

Throughout my life, I'll continue to study God's word, believing and receiving, offering others inklings of those insights that He reveals to me through my studies, the WORD that He places there for me to discover, saturating my heart with the love that He brought to life when Jesus rose from the tomb and destroyed the evil that still tries, unsuccessfully, to darken the light that is alive because HE survives!

Yes! I believe and therefore, I speak. . . Jesus used God's word to fight our enemy and I will use God's word to fight this enemy. Without a doubt, with all my heart, I have a faith that only He could have prompted when, at last, I left that dark woman in the grocery store with my final words—'I must go but I will pray for you'. She may be lost, but not one prayer is wasted. Even those prayers I've prayed that seem to have gone unanswered. . . even they make a way for the heart to turn away from the darkness where there is only doubt and pain, where there is only the desperation of a soul who is lost because they're believing the wrong things. Instead of following the light, they follow the dark.

A Prayer and a Promise

Dear Lord, You already know this woman's heart and her reasons for doubting and shunning the love that You brought to us when You came to earth, when You died for us, when You rose to show a love that only God could have brought to us. You are the way, the truth, the life. And, YOU are the only One who can save. You are the answer to every fear, every tear, every year of struggle and strife. You are the light that shines into the darkness and reminds us that You are far brighter than any of the sparkling sins that, when they're bought, are realized to be what they truly are—filthy, dingy things—things that bring nothing but guilt and shame. Because of YOU, sweet Jesus, I know that I have a second chance to be the person You created me to be, the person who loves, the person

Day Thirty-Six

who sees past the shadows into the music that is a tune only You could play, a beautiful only You could have made, a love that only You could have designed. Thank You, Jesus—for this light so alive!

> Faith is the strength by which a shattered world shall emerge into the light.
> —Helen Keller

Day Thirty-Seven

Matthew 23:23 Woe unto you, scribes and Pharisees, hypocrites! for ye pay tithe of mint and anise and cummin, and have omitted the weightier matters of the law, judgment, mercy, and faith: these ought ye to have done, and not to leave the other undone.

When I pray, I usually ask for God's forgiveness. I don't ask for forgiveness because I'm wallowing in sins of the flesh or sins that are easily named and noticed. I ask for forgiveness because of those sins that often lie secreted within—sometimes buried so deeply that even I, the sinner, fail to notice them. They are sins of doubt and greed, sins of selfishness and discouragement, sins who are sometimes silent but always deadly. They are sins that I might not admit when I pray for forgiveness because they're so deeply planted in my spirit that I actually fail to discern they're inside me. But, they are there and they're scattering shadows of sorrow, shadows of doubt, shadows of darkness, wherever they touch down inside of me. They are hidden, even from me at times, but when I pray—even if I don't notice them, I pray like the publican of Luke 18:13, for God to be merciful to me a sinner.

It's those little sins that rest in our souls who reach through our joys and find ways to disrupt the elations with feelings of discouragement and sadness. Those little sins that often aren't seen because they're quietly brooding within are usually the very sins that leave

Day Thirty-Seven

us feeling like we're not getting anywhere when we pray, when we read the word, when we seek out the guidance of the Lord with our heart's song. We're not failures because we're sinners. That is a given. We're failures because we're not fully repentant. We are not repenting of the sins that seem so little, so hidden, so minute, that we don't even realize we're omitting them from our hearts and spirits.

Just like this verse details, we can so easily become those scribes and Pharisees, paying our tithes and giving to others which in and of itself are good things—but, we are ignoring those things within us that need discovery and direction and repentance. While we do those little things, following the traditions and the letter of the law, we overlook the need to love with our hearts, to love with our spirits, to love with a love that Jesus died so we might experience. His love is the one thing that we're most in need of and His love is the one reason that God made a way for us. Love like Jesus! Give like Jesus! Repent and believe in the light who came to give us the ability to shine our love into the world where darkness would like to cover our sins but where our hearts, flowing with the love that Jesus revealed, exposes the sin for what it is and reassures us that, when we repent—He will certainly forgive us for all our sins and silence every doubt that might cling to our spirits.

We're no different than those scribes and Pharisees. We struggle with faith. And, even though we would like to ignore the worst things about ourselves, we are hypocrites. We read our bibles and pray. We give to the needy and plead with God for healing. We listen to the preacher and congratulate ourselves on being saved. But, so many times we fail to really listen. We fail to hear what God is saying to our spirits. We ignore the little sins that penetrate our souls and work on cleaning up the things that others see in us. While we might like to keep ignoring those sins that aren't shown to the rest of the world, we are certainly much better Christians when we reach out to God with repentant hearts and ask Him to help us to see what we sometimes fail to see, to repent of those sins we so easily forget, to seek His forgiveness and offer His kindness, His light, His love, wherever we are able to.

A Prayer and a Promise

Dear Lord Jesus, You know about all those sins that stay hidden inside, the ones that I would like to ignore as if they don't even exist. You know the worst of my heart and soul and, despite me, You offer me forgiveness and love that is more beautiful than anything I've ever dreamed. You are the light that helps me to see beyond myself into the eyes of those who you've given me to love and care for. You shine a light of love through me that I could never have imagined might come from this heart of mine. You made me better than I could have ever been, and throughout all that is, You keep molding me into someone that can love and I'm learning to love the way that You love because YOU are the Creator and even though I was born many years ago—I am still being created by the love that reflects the meaning of being born again. Thank You, Jesus, for making me better and showing me that I still need to repent, to grow, to reach out to You with a heart who is willing to hear, to learn, to ask for the forgiveness You are famous for giving. Thank You, Jesus. I love YOU!

> To trust God in the light is nothing, but trust Him in the dark—that is faith
> —C.H. Spurgeon

Day Thirty-Eight

Matthew 16:8 Which when Jesus perceived, he said unto them, O ye of little faith, why reason ye among yourselves, because ye have brought no bread?

Yes, I have caught myself worrying and wondering when all I had to do is trust the God who made me, saved me and continues to provide for me—not just the little things that I have need of, but huge things, miraculous things, things that I can't explain away as anything other than what they are. Not only are these things major blessings. They are major miracles, gestures of God's nature, gifts that make me realize I'm not just talking to anyone when I pray. I'm praying to the One who knew me from my mother's womb, the One who silenced every fear that haunted my soul, the One who abides with me and shines His light so that I never need to fear the darkness that sometimes surrounds me. He is the ONE I depend on, the One I yearn to know better, the One whose grace saved me from the depths of despair and the darkest hell that I could possibly imagine.

God fights away my fears with His comforting. He fights away the demons that sometimes prevent me from walking in the light. He fights my spiritual battles when I'm lost in a world of doubt and confusion. He hears my heart, welcomes my prayers, and assures me that as long as He is—and HE IS ETERNAL—I never need to find the way on my own. He is always with me, always blessing me, always protecting me. He is the answer to every fear, the silence in every calm, the beautiful in each star. He quiets my heart when it beats the wildest. He soothes my spirit when it feels like I can't move past the fear. He hushes even those voices in my head that keep me from listening to His still, small voice when He tells me that I am HIS. YES. I am HIS. And, that means I never have to worry about anything. Not ever. His love is alive, limitless and more amazing that anything I might possibly imagine.

When Jesus told His disciples that their faith was so small He knew, already, what they were thinking, what they were in need of, what the very next moment held waiting. Jesus knew. Just like He knew when He was praying before He was arrested—exactly what was waiting for Him. He even prayed that the cup be taken from Him but, nonetheless, for God's will to be done. HE KNEW. Can you imagine knowing that you were going to be beaten, humiliated and die a horrific death on a cross and still going to meet with those who were about to arrest you? Can you possibly imagine— the temptation that must have moved through Him because HE also knew that He could call all the angels of heaven to be at His disposal? He could have ended it all with one word, one look, one inkling of a prayer. He could have let us go to hell. He could have saved Himself!

But, He did not. He chose the nails. He chose the cross. He chose the most painful of deaths. He chose to save the very souls who were torturing and degrading Him with their punishments. Jesus is and will forever be—the greatest man—the greatest teacher—the only Son of God—and the only One capable of hanging on that tree without calling down those angels to destroy all chance for you and me. Jesus truly is the only One who could have done what He did, who could have loved the way He loved, who could have hung on a cross while the world looked on—destroying the evil that raged beyond human eyes, the evil that was so sure it had won because, after all, there on that cross hung the only chance God had—His Son was being put to death!

But, just look what love has done. Just look at God's Son. Just look beyond the foot of the cross to the empty tomb and remember what was won when Jesus assured His followers that He was going

Day Thirty-Eight

to His Father and He'd send a comforter, that same comforter that is stirring my heart to write these very words. Just look what He has done. Just look what He has done. And, it has only just begun!

A Prayer and a Promise

Dear Lord, YOU knew what was to come when they came to arrest You. You knew and still, You went peacefully. You didn't call down the angels or urge God to save You from the fate that meant the worst pain, the worst death. You taught the world what it means to love without conditions, to love in a way that is beyond comprehension, to love so much that there is nothing else I can say or hope or believe... except I love You, Jesus. You are everything to me.

> The Bible teaches that faith is the only approach that we have to God. No man has sins forgiven, no man goes to heaven, no man has assurance of peace and happiness, until he has faith in Jesus Christ.
> —Billy Graham

Day Thirty-Nine

Hebrews 13:7 Remember them which have the rule over you, who have spoken unto you the word of God: whose faith follow, considering the end of their conversation.

I've known many Christian leaders. Some were loud. Some were quiet. Some were gentle and some were outspoken. Some were blessed with wisdom that encouraged. But all were sanctified by the One who brings us hope and joy, peace and fulfillment, a chance to be like Him, the whole reason that I have for writing this devotional.

Yes, I've known so many Christian leaders. And, the ones I remember the best are the ones that reminded me to follow Jesus even when I doubt. They assured me that His grace was worth more than all the 'things' I might attain. They taught me that the light He radiates is a light far more gentle, joyous and sincere than any light that comes from the morning sun. He is the SON that pours out faith to those who need to silence their fears and put distance between the shadows and the promises that He vows.

He is a promise maker—not a promise breaker. When He gives us His word—the Bible—He gives us God breathed promises and guidelines, God breathed wisdoms and ways, God breathed words on these pages that remind us we are children of light—the light that glows from the One named Jesus, the One who saves

Day Thirty-Nine

souls and offers relief from the darkness that surrounds those who are trying to walk without His hand in theirs.

Those Christian leaders that I will always remember the best weren't perfect people. They didn't teach me that I had to be perfect to be a child of God. But they did teach me I had to have a real and sure relationship with the King of Kings. I learned from each one of them, but the thing that all of them were best at saying was "Jesus is the answer" whatever question I might have. "Jesus is the truth" even when I'm unsure of the way. "Jesus is the reason" I have the opportunity and faith to say—Thank You, Jesus, for Your saving grace!

I know that these Christian leaders meant to lead me into a right relationship with God and the best way they did this was by showing me, through their own living, that they sincerely believed what they were saying. They didn't just instruct me on how to live my life or how to live for Christ—although they did do these two things. They lived in such a way that I couldn't doubt they were saved by grace and I wasn't afraid so long as they led the way because the road they were taking was the road to my Savior, the road of faith, the road that was blessed by His sweet grace.

Christian leaders may make mistakes. They don't always know the answers. They may have grating characteristics. They aren't perfect but they are following the One who is and this makes all the difference in the way their life has gone. Because they know Jesus, because they love with a love that He radiates, because they're sincerely praying and praising, there is never any reason to question their leadership. They are the blessings that God gave to us when He saved us. They are the blessings who silence our fears, wipe away our tears, and restore our hearts with the assurance that faith in Jesus is the only thing we need to walk through this life and into eternity with the promise that God's love will always surround us. God's light will shine through our lives, forever. We'll always be children of the One who created us for a purpose.

Pearls of Faith

A Prayer and a Promise

Dear Lord, You knew me in my mother's womb. You know when I fail and when I succeed. You know when I doubt and when I believe. You know when I long to open my heart and share the truth of Your love with a lost and dying world. You know that, through the love that You inspire in me, there is a fire that can't be put out by the darkest fears or tears. You make living a better place to be and You make dying, fearlessly, possible for me. You are the way, the truth and the life. And, I come to You with a heart that knows You are my hope and I'll forever yearn for You. I can't wait to meet You in person. In that moment, I'm not sure what I'll do or what I'll be thinking. . . But above all, I believe I'll be praising—forevermore. Thank You, Jesus. I love You with all my heart.

> Faith is not believing in my own unshakable belief. Faith is believing an unshakable God when everything in me trembles and quakes.
> —Beth Moore

Day Forty

Matthew 17:20 And Jesus said unto them, Because of your unbelief: for verily I say unto you, If ye have faith as a grain of mustard seed, ye shall say unto this mountain, Remove hence to yonder place; and it shall remove; and nothing shall be impossible unto you.

Though the preceding verse isn't my favorite verse in the Bible and I don't call it 'my verse' for living, it easily could be. I first heard this verse when I was quite young and it was probably my mom who first explained the verse to me. Because she had a necklace with a small bauble which held a mustard seed, I'm almost sure she was the first to tell me about this bible verse.

Once I knew the meaning of the verse, the strength of even a little faith, faith the size of a mustard seed, I wanted a necklace like hers. I was amazed that even such a small faith could move a mountain and sometimes wondered about the possibility of moving a mountain. Wow! Amazing faith! Faith that I hoped I was capable of. Faith that I hoped would lead me through this world. Faith in Jesus, who was the strength that left me feeling assured that whatever comes, whatever I'm facing, whatever doubts or failures, I have the answer in the One who lived and died and rose again. The One who came to this earth to be the sacrifice for all of us. Only faith in Jesus could bring me through this world and into the presence of One who would be the light for my heart, eternally.

Pearls of Faith

When I was young, I lost a dog who I loved. No one except me and God knew, but I prayed passionately (for a child) for the dog to come back home. I prayed in faith but, despite my prayers, this dog never returned. Was my faith dented? Probably a little. But that dent didn't discourage me enough to keep me from reaching out to the One who created me—over and over again—with a faith that only He could have introduced in me when I first realized that He is the answer to every need, the joy in every smile, the gentle in every heart and the promise that love will surely silence the darkness that comes from doubt.

All the little 'lost dog' prayers I've prayed—even though they weren't always answered with an affirmative reply—were merely further support of my faith. When I pray, praise or prepare my heart for believing despite the worst doubts, there is the assurance that, with God, even the wildest imaginings become possible. He is a mountain mover. He is a faith builder. He is the reason I can see that just a little faith, faith like a mustard seed, is enough for me.

Though I want a big faith, faith that can truly move the heart of my Savior, I know that I won't always be capable of fully believing every prayer or promise will be answered the way I want them to be. I may have extraordinary faith, faith that will move mountains, but God is in control and God always knows the best answers. So even when the answer is no or wait, I know that I have been answered and God is still blessing me with the best for my soul.

My faith isn't always perfectly believing. But my faith is always the reason I can see through the fear into the wonder of a love that is more beautiful than any earthly love. This agape love is a love that reminds me this verse is so true. Even faith as small as a mustard seed is enough to take me from the darkness to the light, from the hard heart to the soft, from the fear to the trust. Because He gave me faith enough to believe He is my Savior, I can be sure that my heart is blood bought and wherever I go, I will always know that He is with me and His love is surrounding me with hope, joy, peace and every good thing. Because my faith is in Jesus, I have faith that is stronger than I might dream of without His Holy Spirit's leading.

Day Forty

A Prayer and a Promise

Dear Lord, I'm so thankful that You gave me all the faith I need to believe that You are the One who came to show me that grace, that light, that love that will always bring me through the doubts. Because You are the Savior of my soul, I will forever know that I am blessed beyond words. I am blessed in ways that I can't possibly describe with blessings that come from the faith that keeps growing because of Your sacrifice. I have faith in YOU, Lord and I can never thank You, praise You, worship You enough to express how much You mean to me, Jesus. I love You and want You to know that You are the One I will always adore.

> Faith is the avenue to salvation. Not intellectual understanding. Not money. Not your works. Just simple faith. How much faith? The faith of a mustard seed, so small you can hardly see it. But if you will put that little faith in the person of Jesus, your life will be changed. He will come with supernatural power into your heart. It can happen to you.
> —Billy Graham

Wonders

By Regina McIntosh

There's something about dew, glistening,
    Wistful and wishing,
        Clinging to quiet petals,
            Gently hugging...

There's something about mist, indefinable,
    Hazy as a shadow,
        Haunting the heart,
            Heavy with hope...

There's something about shafts of light,
    Creating a trembling desire,
        Coloring the spirit fiery,
            Urging reflections, rising...

There's something about stars, glistening,
    Trembling in the skies,
        Singing joy through the night,
            Falling, smiling, exciting...

There's something about a song, inspiring,
    Drifting through the heart,
        Flowing joy into the soul,
            Harmony that won't let go...

There's something about rain, lightly kissing,
    Stirring the soul to a brave,
        Beyond the fear,
            Aching, daring, audacious...

Day Forty

There's something about silence, tempting,
    Heartening the colors who last,
        Sensations of blue, azure,
            Like the seas, shores so true. . .

There's something about a bible, wisdom,
    Poured out on the one who looks,
        Between the pages, the ages,
            Discovering its truth, so amazing. . .

There's something about His presence,
    It feels like love overflowing,
        Grace that is softly glowing,
            Stirring the melody of His calling. . .

There's something about this pen,
    When it seeks only Him,
        Joy falls in inky shimmers,
            Reflecting a love that is indispensable. . .

There's something about the simple things,
    The music, the trees, the heart who believes,
        When time ends and life stands still,
            There is the promise of eternal peace. . .

There's something about living for God,
    Hearts are blessed beyond words,
        Seeking Him is worth all the hurt,
            He is the One who transforms bad to good. . .

There's something about knowing Jesus,
    Restoring the heart with His reasons,
        To live with the hope of eternity,
            Beside the One who is so worthy. . .

There's something about every living thing,
　Wherever I look, I find His creativity,
　　Signs that He is and He will forever be,
　　　The answer, the light, the love that I need...

I'm so thankful to know the One who lived and died for me!

Conclusion

Whether performed during Easter or Christmas, Messiah, with its powerful "Hallelujah Chorus," has unquestionably been used as a means to evangelize and spread the gospel to a wide audience. Moreover, the message of Messiah has served as a source of inspiration for millions of people, compelling them to donate to those in need, all in the name of Christ. Most composers from that era never expected their music would endure beyond their lifetime. Handel's Messiah is certainly the outlier, being perhaps the oldest continuously performed composition from any composer. Yet George Frideric Handel refused to take the credit. In a beautiful gesture, at the end of Messiah, Handel paid homage to his faith by including the letters "SDG" for Soli Deo Gloria, which means "To God Alone the Glory."[1]

Thus, I'm ending each of my books with the letters "SDG" for Soli Deo Gloria, which means "To God Alone the Glory."

---

1. Vermilye, Alan. *The Hymns of Easter: Daily Lent and Easter Devotions on Classic Hymns (40 Daily Devotions for Lent and Easter)*, The Devotional Hymn Series (Brown Chair Books, Kindle), loc. 18–19.

SDG

www.ingramcontent.com/pod-product-compliance
Lightning Source LLC
Chambersburg PA
CBHW070454090426
42735CB00012B/2543